The Signs of the Times,

the New Ark,

and

the Coming Kingdom of the Divine Will

+++

God's Plan for Victory and Peace

by

Kelly Bowring

When it is evening, you say,
"It will be fair weather; for the sky is red." And in the morning,
"It will be stormy today, for the sky is red and threatening."
You know how to interpret the appearance of the sky,
*but you cannot interpret **the signs of the times**.*
Jesus in Matthew 16:2-3

Library of Congress Control Number: 2013951896
Printed in the United States of America

ISBN-13: 978-0-9802292-4-0
ISBN-10: 0-9802292-4-3

Note from the Publisher: All of the materials used in this book are from Church-approved sources or from sources that have at least received the Church's imprimatur.

To order more copies of this book or the ebook, go to
www.TwoHeartsPress.com
or call toll-free (24/7):
1-800-BookLog (266-5564).

Two Hearts Press

TABLE OF CONTENTS

Only Approved Sources Used in This Book
All the sources used in this book are from only Church approved or
recognized sources, or that have at least received the imprimatur:

Holy Bible

The Catechism (CCC)

St. Francis of Assisi

St. Thomas Aquinas

St. Margaret Mary

St. Louis de Montfort

St. John Eudes

St. Hannibal De Francia

Servant of God Luisa Piccarreta

Bl. Anna Maria Taigi

Bl. Elizabeth of the Trinity

Ven. "Conchita" (Concepion Cabrera de Armida)

Bl. Dina Belanger

St. Alphonsus Liguori

St. Nicholas von Flue

Ven. Mary of Agreda

St. John Bosco

St. Catherine Labouré

St. Hildegard

Bl. Elizabeth Canori Mora

Bl. Anne Catherine Emmerich

Ven. Magdalene Porzat

Visionaries of Fatima

Servant of God Cora Evans

Bl. Elena Aiello

St. Maximilian Kolbe

St. Faustina Kowalska

Ven. Fulton Sheen

St. Pio

Servant of God Maria Esperanza

Pope Leo XIII

St. Pius X

Ven. Pius XII

Pope Paul VI

St. John Paul II

Pope Benedict XVI

Our Lady of Guadalupe

Our Lady of Good Success

Our Lady of the Miraculous Medal

Our Lady of La Salette

Our Lady of Heede

Our Lady of Fatima

Mediatrix of All Grace

The Virgin of Cuapa

Our Lady of Akita

Our Lady of America

Our Lady of All Nations

Our Lady of Good Help

The Sorrowful and Immaculate Heart of Mary

The Flame of Love of the Immaculate Heart of Mary

PREFACE

It was Saturday, October 13, 2012, and I was woken up suddenly at 5:45a.m. by a familiar motherly voice, which instructed me to get up and go to the window of the hotel room and look outside to see *"the sign"*. As I opened the curtain, I saw the **Morning Star** (Venus) straight out high in the eastern sky. Directly below it was the brightly illuminated, very beautiful **crescent moon** (facing upward). And straight below it on the horizon was the still faint, dawning light of the **rising sun** about to announce the new day. Moving in the Spirit, I knew this was a sign from above. I understood this sign was a gift to me from Our Lady. And it was especially for me. A few moments later, as the heavenly constellations shifted, the sign was gone. I had been stirred and directed to see it at a perfect moment, and the sight made me feel overwhelmed with a sense of God's presence and love.

Though I did not remember it at the time, about nine days previously I had begun a novena asking the Lord and His Mother whether this work of spreading **the heavenly Message** of our times was important, whether I was cut out for it (or could survive it), and whether God wanted me to continue doing this work as part of His Will. As a confirmation to my novena's intention, I had been asking Our Lady for **a double sign** – for literally two signs that were distinct but the same, to confirm that this was God's plan for me. I did not know what I was asking for or what kind of signs I might receive. And on this morning, I had not connected the sign in the sky I received with the novena or its intention. Not yet.

I spent that weekend in mid-October speaking at a diocesan conference in Fargo, North Dakota, this being my first time there. And it was a blessed and fruitful weekend. After the conference, before I flew home on Monday morning, I woke up early before dawn to walk to morning Mass at the cathedral. There was no sign of the moon now, and the sun was not yet dawning. All was chilly and dark. So, I was on my own, or so I thought. On my way through downtown, I came across two men standing in front of a closed building. As I walked by, they said: *"Good morning, Dr. Bowring."* Surprised, I soon learned they had attended the conference and were up early praying in front of an abortion clinic. Wondering what I was doing there, I explained to them that I was on my way to Mass. They told me I would never make it, as I was going in the wrong direction. So, redirected with their guardian-angel-like help, I made it to the Cathedral of St. Mary as Mass began. After Mass I stayed to pray the Rosary.

In the middle of the Rosary, with my head lowered, I heard the same voice that had spoken to me the earlier morning, which now said gently: *"Kelly, look up. I have the second sign for you."* As I was listening to the voice, at that moment I recalled my previous request for a double sign as part of my prior week's novena; and I now had a clear sense that I was being given the second sign as confirmation of that prayer. So I looked up seeing the altar area… and there was the sign. I saw **a star** among several stars high on the wall behind the altar, below it was the image of Mary standing on **a crescent moon**, and below this was the tabernacle with a light shining on it causing a radiant glow that made it look like **a rising sun**. It was the exact sign I had seen in the sky the morning of two days prior, but now with more religious significance. I was both stunned and filled with joy. I had now received two signs as requested – a sign from nature and a sign from grace, both distinct yet both the same, and both given from above. My prayer was answered in a way I could not have imagined.

And I knew what this meant. I was being called to continue proclaiming the heavenly Message of our times. And I believe you are as well. **This book is about the heavenly Messages, Warnings, and Signs of our times**, which are coming to us today from the heart of the Church through the Popes, Saints and Mystics, and from the Hearts of Jesus and Mary. The truth is that God is speaking to the world and He desires to give us extra graces to prepare us for the New Era of Peace.

I think that God wants you to realize that each of you reading the Message of this book is being called by Our Lady, who is standing on the moon as the New Ark, and who is coming from Heaven today to prepare us for the New Era of her Son, which is just on the horizon of our time. **This is a Message of hope!** And like the Morning Star, God wants us to be a light for others and to be one of His signs of hope in these times. This is not about the end of the world, but about a new Kingdom about to dawn for the world. I hope you enjoy this book! And please share it with others because the world today, overwhelmed by darkness where falsehood seems to prevail, needs urgently to hear the 'good news' that a new unending day of Christ is indeed dawning and is almost here. And – as you will see discussed in this book – through *"The Signs of the Times"* that are becoming increasingly evident today, God is showing us the time is now!

CHAPTER 1

Jesus Spoke of These Times in Scripture –
About the End Times & the New Kingdom on Earth

Jesus said to his disciples:
Beware that your hearts do not become drowsy
from carousing and drunkenness
and the anxieties of daily life,
*and **that day** catch you by surprise like a trap.*
*For **that day** will assault everyone*
who lives on the face of the earth.
***Be vigilant** at all times*
***and pray** that you have the strength*
to escape the tribulations that are imminent
and to stand before the Son of Man.
Luke 21:34-36

*Blessed are those who **listen to this <u>prophetic message</u>***
*and **heed what is written in it**, for the appointed time is near.*
Revelation 1:1-4

What is **God's Plan** for our times – concerning what is going
on in the world, why God is allowing the rise of evil and even
planning world-wide chastisements Himself, how we can make it
through these turbulent times safely, and about what is on the other

side of this time of upheaval and darkness? This book answers that question. This is not an end-of-the-world book calling for its readers to engage in radical acts of self-preservation (though some might feel called to do that on their own). This book is about so much more than that! It is about **the Grace of all graces**, that of forming in you God's **Divine Will** and then of preparing for His Kingdom for the benefit of the whole human family. This book acknowledges that we are living in times worse than the time of the Flood, and that God is again today offering us an ark to bring us through these times to safety and victory; but this time **the Ark** is not a boat, but a heart. It is the Heart of His Mother. Mary is Our Lady of Hope, especially in the midst of war! This book is about hope! This book shows the road to peace! So the question is: Do you want to know what God's Plan is? Not only does He have a Plan, but He assures the Victory as well. Read on and see!

In God Is My Safety and My Glory!

This book intends to call you to great courage, to warn you of the times at hand, and to discuss God's Plan in order that He can prepare you (and the world) for the New Kingdom. And **the two means** to receive this Gift and to get to the new Era of Peace are:

1) For you to pass through this time of the great battle in **the New Ark of safety and protection**, via Devotion and Consecration to the Immaculate Heart of Mary; and

2) For you to learn about and enter into **the glory of living in the Divine Will** now and pray for **the coming Kingdom of**

the **Divine Will**, which will come soon hereafter for the whole world. Yes, there are two gifts God is preparing to give – one to each of us and one to the whole world:

- **For each of you** right now: the Grace of all graces – the invitation for you to live in the Divine Will, beginning right now; and

- **For the whole world** after this time of distress and transition – the New Era of Peace, which will usher in the Kingdom of the Divine Will on earth as it is in Heaven.

This is **the secret of all secrets** that God has been revealing to us for our times – hidden in Scripture, prepared by His Saints, and now fully given to us as the time of fulfillment is at hand. But, we must be careful to approach this Message with humility and with a welcoming and child-like spirit; for the Lord has *"hidden these things from the wise and the learned [and] revealed them [only] to the childlike"* (Matthew 11:25). So, now it is time to learn the 'good news' of the heavenly Message of our times, to step into the New Ark, and to begin living renewed in the Divine Will, while preparing for **the New Era** that will soon dawn on the other side of this *"greatest historical confrontation"* (John Paul II) and spiritual battle in human history.

The secret is to trust in the Lord and His Plan. Come along now and see. The purpose of this Book is to explain to you about **the greatest Grace God has ever given humanity**, to understand and live in this Grace, and to move safely through these times to the new era where this Grace will be given to all humanity. The reality of when the merciful chastisements unfold is not of importance simply in itself, but should be seen in light of their purpose – **to prepare the world for the new Era of Grace, the Kingdom of the Divine Will**. Whether we are talking about the prophecies of Fatima, Akita, or Budapest, the big picture of all these revelations is to tell us about and prepare us for the new era of the universal establishing of the Divine Will and to guide us to cross these times of transition in the New Ark.

God has indicated the great battle and chastisements have begun, and they must continue because mankind has not responded to His warnings to return to Him and to reject sin. God wants to save humanity, so He is chastising us. But, He wants to protect His faithful as well. A critical reality at the heart of the heavenly messages of our times is that God has declared it in advance and has given us **the sure way to victory and safety**; and that you should want this new Grace He is offering in and of itself, both for yourselves and for the whole world. The secret now revealed is the fact that **this Grace exists** and that you would be like the foolish virgins if you did not accept the most extraordinary grace ever offered to help in your salvation in these times and achieve the highest possible glory in Heaven.

Jesus died in order to save humanity and to give us eternal life. He freed all souls from bondage to the devil and to sin. The only way to Eternal Life is through Jesus Christ. Because He is so merciful, He allows everyone the chance to come to Him, by their own free will. He gave the world the Truth and, by His death on the Cross, He opened the way for all to live in eternal peace. We must remember that **victory in this battle belongs to Christ**. Love will conquer all. We love

Christ. He loves us and gives us supernatural grace. In these times, we need to rely on the love of Christ to withstand and dispel the darkness; and like a beacon our love will attract other souls. This is the way of Our Lady. She is the *"moon"* that reflects the love of the *"sun"* who is Christ, and thus vanquishes the darkness of the night. So, too, must we share the love of Christ in these times to help save souls, as *"stars"* to dispel the darkness of our times, and to bring others to the horizon where the New Day is already dawning! It does not matter that many today sneer at this Message to prepare us for the Great Day. In time they will know it is Jesus Christ and His Mother who are coming to us.

The New Ark of Safety and Victory

There is plenty written already on why the chastisements must come and why the final battle is unfolding today. The heavenly Plan is unfolding as the great battle ensues, and it involves Satan and his enemy, the **Woman of Revelation** who will crush his head with her heel. It has been declared from the beginning: *"I will put enmity between you and the Woman; between your offspring and hers"* (Genesis 3:15). Our job is to make sure we are on the side of the Woman, under her patronage, through consecration to her Immaculate Heart. For, *"She will crush [Satan's] head as he makes an attempt on her heel"* (Genesis 3:15). Just as Mary conquered in her Fiat – *"Let it be done to me according to Your Word"* (Luke 1:46) – when by her "yes" the Word was made flesh in her womb, and when she said *"yes"* to her Son's death on the Cross at Calvary, she continues today, **coming from Heaven and gathering her spiritual *offspring* to say** *"yes"* **to the divine Plan.** The main purpose of this book is in discussing the great Grace of the Divine Will itself and about the aftermath of the great battle, what the battle will bring – the new era of the Kingdom of the Divine Will and the ultimate fulfillment of the Our Father petition where we pray: Thy Kingdom Come, Thy Will be done, on earth as it is in Heaven.   Our Lady is gathering her spiritual children today in this final battle to reflect all her glory in them, so that she and her offspring can bring victory and usher in the New Era of Peace. She has chosen *you* to join her and her Son in this fight, as the new apostles of these latter times to help save the world.

The New Grace and Kingdom

Jesus reveals to us in the Lord's Prayer that we are called to find fulfillment in desiring the holy will of God, as we pray: Thy Will be done on earth as it is in Heaven. We are called to seek the heavenly and spiritual things first, as Jesus says: *"Seek ye first the Kingdom of God and His righteousness, and all else shall be given to you"* (Matthew 6:33). And while it is all good to seek to surrender to God's will, it is altogether greater to learn about the Grace of all graces whereby **God is now calling us to live in His Divine Will itself**, which contains all truths, all loves, all sanctities, all beauty, all goodness, all wisdom. That is why living in the Divine Will is *"the greatest miracle"* and the perfect development of divine life (grace) in the creature. For in this, His Divine Will divinizes and operates Itself in our human will. This book will discuss this new Grace and the new Era, and how this new Grace will protect you from the chastisements as God wills it and will even more offer you **the Sanctity of all sanctities** now, as the first fruits of the new Kingdom to come on Earth in the very short and near future.

This Grace of all graces is not simply about doing or following God's Will, but *living in* **God's Will**. The earth is an exile for those who do not do or live in God's Will. What is important for you as we begin, is that you make every effort to have a good disposition to receive so great a good. But, for those who say *"yes"* to living in God's Will, as it is in Heaven so it is on earth for them. In this, God enters our will with His Divine Will so that we are filled to the brim with His goods, giving us joys and happiness without number. He gives us dominion over ourselves, converts our passions into virtue, and our weaknesses into divine fortitude. Whereas, for one to live on his own apart from the Divine Will, as most do now, the virtues they exercise are forced and inconsistent, and all the while being enslaved by their own miseries, thus in a general state of unhappiness. By beginning to live in the Divine Will, you **enter the new Kingdom itself**, and help to bring about the Kingdom of the Divine Will on earth as it is in Heaven, which will herald the New Era of Peace as the new sun that will dispel the clouds of all evils. So God has chosen you with the unique purpose of forming in you the glory of His Kingdom by calling you to live in the Divine Will, so that through you He can form the Kingdom of His Will upon the Earth (as it already is in Heaven), which is His complete glory. What happiness awaits you; what glory too! Say: *"Jesus, remember me when You come into Your Kingdom!"*

Using Only Approved Sources

To make this discussion more solid and reasonable, in this book we will use only sources that have the Church's approval or at least have received an imprimatur of recognition as solid and reliable. Thus, the presentation of this book's themes are so **remarkably credible**, while the sheer multiplicity of sources, which all agree with one another, each adding a new detail to the divine puzzle of God's Great Plan, all fit together to make up **one complete indisputable picture of the signs of our times** – makes the Message of this book so overwhelmingly powerful and convincing. This is a book of the most solid sources of the Church, organized and presented systematically without speculation and without unneeded fanfare. **This book is for every audience, for everyone, and certainly for *you*.** It discusses **the most important Message** from God to the world in these times – even since the time of Christ. Oh, if you only knew what awaits you! Read on, and give this book your greatest attention. There is no greater gift, no greater good news, no greater revelation for our times. Here it is; read on and receive all that God has in store for you, for you **right now**! I suggest by my own experience that the best approach to reading this book is to read it in prayer, even as a prayer, and to meditate on its content and the various sources it uses, putting into practice what it offers. Then, *you* will benefit greatly from what it offers – entering the New Ark and receiving the Grace of all graces yourself. There can be nothing more wonderful in store for you!

Foundations in Scripture

Let's begin by laying a foundation to God's Plan as we look at some related Scripture. In Ephesians 3:14-21 St. Paul discusses God's future plans:

> *For this reason I kneel before the Father... that he may grant you in accord with the riches of his glory **to be strengthened with power through his Spirit in the inner self**, and that **Christ may dwell in your hearts** through faith; that you, rooted and grounded in love, may have strength to comprehend with all the holy ones what is the breadth and length and height and depth, and to know the love of Christ that surpasses knowledge, **so that you may be filled with all the fullness of God**.*

St. Paul further emphasizes God's unfolding plan into the future in Ephesians 4:11-16:

> *And he gave some as apostles, others as prophets, others as evangelists, others as pastors and teachers, to equip the holy ones for the work of ministry, for building up the body of Christ, **until we all attain to the unity of faith and knowledge of the Son of God**, to mature manhood, to the extent of the full stature of Christ, so that we may no longer be infants... Rather, living the truth in love, **we should grow in every way into him** who is the head, Christ.*

Paul likewise discusses this new grace in Colossians 1:27-29:

> *...**the mystery hidden** from ages and from generations past. But now it has been manifested to his holy ones, to whom God chose to make known the riches of the glory of this mystery*

among the Gentiles; it is Christ in you, the hope for glory. It is he whom we proclaim, admonishing everyone and teaching everyone with all wisdom, that we may present everyone perfect in Christ. For this I labor and struggle, in accord with the exercise of his power working within me.

These three Scripture passages all point to the new Grace of the Divine Will dwelling in our soul and transforming our lives to becoming perfect in Christ.

The Church Lives the Life of Christ

Before the new Era of Peace arrives as promised at Fatima, the Church must follow the Lord's own chronology of His life on earth. The Church must endure her crucifixion, so as to rise with Christ into the new Era of Peace. As the **Catechism** states: *"Before Christ's second coming, the Church must pass through a final trial that will shake the faith of many believers... The Church will enter the glory of the Kingdom only through this final passion, when she will follow her Lord in his death and resurrection"* (675-7). This final trial will wake up, purify, and renew humanity to receive the Second Coming and enter the New Kingdom! And Mary's role today, as the Mother of the Body of Christ the Church, is to stand with us in this final crucifixion.

Recently, Pope Benedict XVI reemphasized this truth: *"The Church walks the same path and suffers the same destiny as Christ... she follows the way of the cross, becoming a traveling companion of all humanity. So, in effect, the Church must live the life of Christ, since she is the Bride of the Holy Spirit. Two have become One."*

The World Today

The world is in dire straits today. What does Scripture say about the latter times? About these times? Paul discusses them in his letters to Timothy, saying:

> *Now the Spirit expressly says that **in latter times** some will depart from the faith by <u>giving heed to **deceitful spirits** and doctrines of **demons**</u> through the pretensions of liars... But understand this, that in **the last days** there will come times of stress. For men will be **lovers of self, lovers of money, [and] lovers of pleasure** rather than lovers of God, holding the form of religion but denying the power of it* (1 Timothy 4:1-2, 2 Timothy 3:1-5).

Our times need a divine intervention – to help wake us up, to stop us from going over the precipice of disaster, and to prepare us for the great new grace of the Kingdom of the Divine Will. This was perhaps referred to by Pope John Paul II in his Apostolic Letter *"The Holy Rosary of the Blessed Virgin Mary"*, when it states: *"The grave challenges confronting the world at the start of the new Millennium lead us to think that only **an intervention from on high**, capable of guiding the hearts of those living in situations of conflict and those governing the destinies of nations, can give reason to hope for a brighter future."* Why is God preparing the faithful members of His Church now? God is preparing the remnant who will survive the passion of His Church, because the cruelty of the Beast will be such that great faith, the faith of living in the Divine Will united to the Immaculate Heart of Mary, will be needed to survive this period. This is the secret of secrets of our time; it is the grace of all graces too. Jesus spoke about what was coming, saying:

> **Do not be terrified**... *Nation will rise against nation... there will be great earthquakes, and in various places famines and pestilences; and there will be terrors and **great signs** from heaven... and upon the earth distress of nations in perplexity at the roaring of the sea and the waves, men fainting with fear... for the powers of **the heavens will be shaken*** (Luke 21:9-28).

There will be many casualties in this great battle that will usher in the new era and kingdom to come. As we read in Zechariah Chapter 13: 8-9, *"In all the land, says the Lord, **two-thirds of them shall be cut off and perish**, and one-third shall be left. I will bring the one third through fire, and I will refine them as silver is refined, and I will test them as gold is tested. They shall call upon my name, and I will hear them."* Either we will not make it or we will be refined through fire. Those who will make it will call on the Name of the Lord, enter the New Ark, and seek His Divine Will. For more on the times we are living in, see my other books on this subject: *The Secrets, Chastisement, and Triumph of the Two Hearts* with imprimatur by Cardinal Vidal and *The Great Battle Has Begun* (Two Hearts Press).

All these things will serve to cleanse the world and prepare it for the new kingdom. The Lord has granted a secret of protection to carry us from this side to the other side of these times – it is the New Ark. This is God's plan: The great battle commences, the New Ark is given, victory is assured, the new Kingdom of the Divine Will arrives, an era of peace is granted, and finally, Christ will come again in glory.

Scripture further describes this period to come in which the Lord will judge His people and bring about a transformation of the world, in Isaiah 11:4-11:

> *But **he shall judge** the poor with justice, and decide aright for the land's afflicted. **He shall strike the ruthless** with the rod of his mouth, and with the breath of his lips he shall slay the wicked. Justice shall be the band around his waist, and faithfulness a belt upon his hips. **Then the wolf shall be a guest of the lamb**… The baby shall play by the cobra's den, and the child lay his hand on the adder's lair. There shall be **no harm or ruin** on all my holy mountain; **for the earth shall be filled with knowledge of the Lord**, as water covers the sea.*
>
> *…On that day, **the Lord shall again take it in hand to reclaim the remnant of his people**.*

The people who will keep their faith during the period of the Beast will need extraordinary grace. Some will volunteer to be martyrs for the Faith. How can God bring this about? How will God bring this about? He tells many of the Saints that He has indeed granted a special grace to imitate Him. It is a sharing in the same grace He gave to His Mother. It is the same grace Adam had before the fall. But, for us, it is a *"new grace"*; it is the Grace of all graces.

Our Divine Mission: Defeating Satan and Saving Souls from Hell

We can choose our actions, but we cannot choose our consequences. Just because we think we are all good and fine, does not mean we are; and just because someone does not believe in Hell does not mean they will not end up there. We must consider the consequences of our actions. While God is merciful to the repentant, if we deliberately disobey God's Commandments or the Church's doctrine (or try to re-write them), we will not be saved. For *"Whoever disobeys the Son will not see life, but the wrath of God remains upon him"* (John 3:36) and *"Do you not know that the unjust will not inherit the kingdom of God? Do not be deceived"* (1 Corinthians 6:9). It is helpful to consider the **reality of Hell**. Jesus said it is the 'place' of *"the fiery furnace, where there will be wailing and grinding of teeth"* (Matthew 13:43), a fire that shall never be quenched (Mark 9:48). Our Lady showed **the visionaries of Fatima** a vision of many damned souls and demons that were in Hell. She then gave us a mission to help save persons today who are headed there, saying: *"Pray, **pray a great deal and make many sacrifices** for **many souls go to Hell** because they have no one to make sacrifices and to pray for them."* She then taught them the *"O my Jesus"* prayer to be prayed at the end of each decade of the Rosary. In that prayer, we say: *"... save us from the fires of hell. Lead all souls to Heaven..."*

St. Faustina was also shown a vision of Hell and details about the real and eternal sufferings that occur there. She wrote:

> *I, Sister Faustina Kowalska, by the order of God, have visited the abysses of Hell... I noticed one thing: **That most of the souls there are those who disbelieved that there is a hell.** It is a place of great torture; how awesomely large and extensive it is! The kinds of tortures I saw:*
>
> **The First Torture that constitutes Hell is**: *The loss of God.*

The Second is: Perpetual remorse of conscience.

The Third is: That one's condition will never change.

The Fourth is: The fire that will penetrate the soul without destroying it. A terrible suffering since it is a purely spiritual fire, lit by God's (just) anger.

The Fifth Torture is: Continual darkness and a terrible suffocating smell, and despite the darkness, the devils and the souls of the damned see each other and all the evil, both of others and their own.

The Sixth Torture is: The constant company of Satan.

The Seventh Torture is: Horrible despair, hatred of God, vile words, curses and blasphemies.

*[And] there are special Tortures destined for particular souls. These are the torments of the senses. **Each soul undergoes terrible and indescribable sufferings related to the manner in which it has sinned…***

*Let the sinner know that he **will be tortured throughout all eternity**, in those senses which he made use of to sin. **I am writing this at the command of God, so that no soul may find an excuse by saying there is no hell, or that nobody has ever been there, and so no one can say what it is like…** how terribly souls suffer there! Consequently, I **pray even more fervently for the conversion of sinners**. I incessantly plead God's mercy upon them. O My Jesus, I would rather be in agony until the end of the world, amidst the greatest sufferings, than offend you by the least sin.*

CHAPTER 2

Jesus Unfolds God's Plan about the Latter Times – From the Writings of the Saints and Popes

Let not your heart be disturbed.
Am I not here, who is your Mother?
Are you not under my protection?
Do not grieve nor be disturbed by anything.
Mother Mary to St. Juan Diego

Pray to Me through My Sacred Heart. Through this Heart, will I harken to your prayers and you will obtain whatever you desire.
Jesus to St. Margaret Mary

God has given us many prophecies about the times that are at hand from the writings of the Saints and Popes. A prophecy is a promise that a God makes to humanity – that disposes us to desire and anticipate the promise. His prophecies are divine truths revealing future events (or impending dangers) and His divine will concerning them, how best to handle them, and to help us live more fully in this period of history. Paul says: *"Test everything; hold fast to what is good"* (1 Thess. 5:21).

Sacred Scripture warns that there will be a falling away from faith before the Second Coming (2 Thessalonians 2:3f). The Bible also warns about the Antichrist who will deny Jesus has come in the flesh (2 John 7). The *Catechism of the Catholic Church* confirms some details about the Antichrist, saying he will be a pseudo-messiah glorifying *"himself in the place of God and of his Messiah come in the flesh;"* and it states that his deception will be ***"a religious deception offering men an apparent solution to their problems at the price of apostasy from the truth."*** The *Catechism* also warns that this final trial **will shake the faith of many believers**; many believers will be misled and deceived. The Saints have also offered prophecy concerning the Antichrist, as exemplified by St. Cyril of Jerusalem, who said: *"Antichrist will exceed in malice, perversity, lust, wickedness, impiety, and heartless cruelty and barbarity all men that have ever disgraced human nature... He shall **through his great power, deceit and malice, succeed in decoying or forcing to his worship two-thirds of mankind;** the remaining third part of men will most steadfastly continue true to the faith and worship of Jesus Christ."*

Prophecies of punishments or chastisements are conditional and always remedial. God is not vindictive or vengeful and doesn't want our condemnation but our salvation. God wants us to consider the prophecies of our times, rather than dismiss them or ignore them. Let us look to the prophecies of our times and heed them with hope.

I. TWO FAMOUS PROPHESIES OF THE GREAT BATTLE

The reality has been that prophecy about chastisement does in fact come to fulfillment, as Heaven had previously warned. This is exemplified by King Louis XIV, who did not heed the requests of Jesus through His messages to St. Margaret Mary for the public practice of the Sacred Heart Devotion. Subsequently, the French Revolution broke out 100 years later to the day; and his grandson King Louis XVI and his wife and son were beheaded.

Similarly, the world did not heed the requests of Our Lady of Fatima for prayer and penance. Subsequently, the world suffered from her prophesied chastisements of World War II and the spread of the dictatorship of atheistic communism, both of which resulted in over 100 million deaths. On August 19, 1931, Sister Lucia, one of the Fatima visionaries, said that Jesus appeared to her and made this complaint: *"Make it known to My ministers, given that they follow the example of the King of France in delaying the execution of My command, they will follow him into misfortune. **It is never too late to have recourse to Jesus and Mary.**"* She later wrote in another text, *"Our Lord complained to me, 'They did not wish to heed My request! ... Like the King of France they will repent of it, and they will do it, but it will be late. **Russia will have already spread its errors in the world, provoking wars and persecutions against the Church.** The Holy Father will have much to suffer.'"* When will we listen?! What will it take to wake us up to the present darkness and impending disaster?!

1. St. John Bosco's Dream

It is in the context of our current times that the famous dream of St. John Bosco (1862) becomes clearer than ever. He had a famous vision, one that he described as an allegory. As reported by witnesses who heard him tell it, the vision is as follows:

On the whole surface of the sea you see an infinity of ships...
*There is **a great storm**.*

*Imagine that in the middle of the sea you also see two very tall columns. On one is the statue of the Blessed Virgin Immaculate, with the inscription underneath: "**Help of Christians**". On the other one, which is even bigger and taller, there is a Eucharistic Host of proportionately large size in relation to the column, and under it the words: "**Salvation of believers**". From the base of the column hang many chains with anchors for ships to attach.*

*The bigger ship of the allied fleet that is **under attack** is captained by the Pope, and all his efforts are bent to steer this ship of the Holy See in between those two columns... There is indescribable rejoicing on the enemy ships at the damage they do the Pope's ship. But a breeze blowing from the two columns is enough to heal every wound and close up the holes. The ship again continues on its way. There are during this time two papally summoned conferences of the captains of the allied ships. On the way **the Pope falls once because he had been gravely wounded**, then rises again, is wounded again, falls a second time and **dies**. When he falls the second time, dead, a shout of joy goes up among the remaining enemies. As soon as he is dead, there is a conclave of the allied captains to elect **a new Pope**, and another Pope immediately replaces him. He guides the ship to the two columns.*

Once there, he attaches the ship with one anchor to the column with the consecrated Host, with another anchor to the column with the Immaculate Conception.

*Then **total disorder** breaks out over the whole surface of the sea. All the ships that so far had been battling the Pope's ship scatter, flee, and collide with one another, some foundering and trying to sink the others.*

*Those at a distance keep prudently back until the remains of all the demolished ships have sunk into the depths of the sea, and then they vigorously make their way to the side of the bigger ship. Having joined it, they too attach themselves to the anchors hanging from the two columns and remain there in **perfect calm**, all safe and secure.*

The ship of the Pope and his allied fleet is the Church, of which he is the head. St. John Bosco said that one Pope is wounded and another is later martyred. John Paul II was wounded in 1981; will another Pope be killed? The enemy ships are the persecutions in store for the Church, and the sea is this world. In the final stages, the battle ensues from within the Church herself. Those who were defending the Church are the good people, attached to the Church and true faith; the others are its enemies, who try to destroy it, with wolves in sheep's clothing among them. And the two columns of safety are devotion to Mary Most Holy and to the Most Blessed Sacrament of the Eucharist.

The Marian title *"Help of Christians"* originated from the Christian naval victory over the invading Muslim Turks at Lepanto, on October 7, 1571. Later, the Pope called this feast: Our Lady of the

Most Holy Rosary. The Church now and then will suffer damages, symbolized by the holes made in the big ship by the weapons, but a *"breeze"* from the Almighty and the Blessed Virgin is enough to repair those damages, though with the loss of some souls. The moral, then, is that we have **only two means** to stand firm in this time of confusion: devotion to the Virgin Mary and frequent reception and adoration of the Most Holy Eucharist.

2. St. Hildegard, Newest Doctor of the Church

On May 10, 2012, Pope Benedict XVI extended the liturgical cult of St. Hildegard to the universal Church, in a process known as *"equivalent canonization"*. He also named her the 35th Doctor of the Church in October 2012. This was **the last significant act of his pontificate**, as four months later he retired, which came as a surprise to many. St. Hildegard is most known for her prophecies about the end times. Regarding these times, she prophesied about a comet that will disrupt the normal events of humanity. She wrote:

> Before **the comet** comes, many nations, the good excepted, will be scourged by want and famine...[After the] great Comet, **the great nation will be devastated** by earthquakes, storms, and great waves of water, causing much want and plagues... For in none of those cities does a person live according to the Laws of God. A powerful wind will rise in the North, carrying heavy fog and the densest dust, and it will fill their throats and eyes so that they will cease their butchery and be stricken with a great fear.

St. Hildegard prophesied about the antichrist saying:

*The son of perdition is this very wicked beast who **will put to death those who refuse to believe in him**; who will associate with kings, priests, the great and the rich... who will finally subjugate the entire universe by his diabolic means... Later, however, after the coming of Enoch and Elias, the Antichrist will be destroyed, and the Church will sing forth with unprecedented glory, and the victims of the great error will throng to return to the fold.*

St. Hildegard gave more details about the antichrist in her Vision X:

Nothing good *will enter into him nor be able to be in him... From the beginning of his course many battles and many things contrary to the lawful dispensation will arise, and charity will be extinguished in men... and there will be so **many heresies** that heretics will preach their errors openly and certainly; and there shall be so much doubt and incertitude in the Catholic faith of Christians that men shall be in doubt of what God they invoke, and **many signs** shall appear in the sun and moon, and in the stars and in the waters, and in other elements and creatures...*

*Then within the Christian people **the Holy Godhead will accomplish signs and wonders** as He accomplished them at the time of Moses with the pillar of cloud and as **Michael the Archangel** did when he fought the heathen for the sake of the Christians. Because of Michael's help God's faithful children will march under his protection. They will decimate their foes and achieve victory through God's power...*

But those who are perfect in the Catholic faith will await in great contrition what God wills to ordain. And these great tribulations shall proceed in this way, while the Son of Perdition shall open his mouth in the words of falsehood and his deceptions, heaven and earth shall tremble together. But after the fall of the Antichrist the glory of the Son of God shall be increased... After the sorrowful defeat of the Son of Perdition, the spouse of my Son, who is the Church, will shine with a glory without equal, and the victims of the error will be impressed to reenter the sheepfold.

St. Hildegard also discusses the false prophet, who she prophesies will be an antipope. She explains how he will promote the mark of the beast. She says:

When the other cardinals elect the next pope, [a] cardinal will proclaim himself Anti-pope, and two-thirds of the Christians will go with him.

The mark (of the Beast) will be a hellish symbol of Baptism, because thereby a person will be stamped as an adherent of Antichrist and also of the Devil in that he thereby gives himself over to the influence of Satan. Whoever will not have this mark of Antichrist can neither buy nor sell anything and will be beheaded. He will... subjugate the entire earth.

A False Pope – The False Prophet?

Is it even possible for a false pope or anti-pope to sit in the Chair of Peter, as St. Hildegard prophesies? **Yes, it is plausible**. And even if this were to actually happen in our lifetimes, we must never take it upon ourselves to judge the validity of the Pope. We are *never* personally permitted to believe the Pope is invalid, unless the highest legitimate authority of the Church were to indicate that he is. All **practicing Catholics** must personally declare the following:

1. I accept the teaching of the Universal Catholic Church that the Pope when speaking on faith and morals is infallible. This includes *"all acts of the Magisterium [which] derive from the same source, that is, from Christ... For this same reason, magisterial decisions in matters of discipline, even if they are not guaranteed by the charism of infallibility, are not without divine assistance and call for the adherence of the faithful"* (*Donum Veritatis*), which every member of the Catholic faithful is obliged to offer the Pope.

2. I accept the current Pope as valid.

No matter what, we must remain faithful to the Church and to the authentic Magisterium. But, this does not have to prohibit us from asking whether a Pope, even validly elected, could ever be the false prophet. The answer is – YES.

So, how could it happen that a validly-elected Pope could become the false prophet (an invalid pope or an anti-pope)? Pope Paul IV's Papal Bull *Cum ex Apostolatus Officio* teaches that if anyone was a heretic before the Papal election, he could not be a valid Pope, even if he is (validly) elected unanimously by the Cardinals. As well, Canon 188.4 (1917 Code of Canon Law) states that if a cleric (pope, bishop, etc.) becomes a heretic, he loses his office, without any declaration, by operation of law. Many Saints spoke about this possibility as well. St. Robert Bellarmine, St. Antonius, St. Francis de Sales, St. Alphonsus Liguori, and many other theologians all taught that a heretic cannot be a valid pope, as for example St. Alphonsus Liguori, Church Doctor, who said:

> *If however, God were to permit a pope to become*
>
> *a notoriously and contumacious heretic,*
>
> *he would by such fact cease to be pope,*
>
> *and the apostolic chair would be vacant.*

We might ask similarly whether it is ever acceptable **to criticize** the Pope. Generally it should be avoided, but in certain circumstances, the answer is 'yes'. An example of this was done in Scripture by **St. Paul who confronted Pope St. Peter**, writing about the encounter saying: *"And when Cephas (Pope St. Peter) came to Antioch, I opposed him, before everyone, to his face because he clearly was wrong"* (Galatians 2:11-14). **St. Thomas Aquinas** confirms, saying: *"There being an imminent danger for the Faith, prelates must be questioned, even publicly, by their subjects."* Explaining the correctness of resisting wayward ecclesiastics, even popes, **St. Augustine** writes, *"It is possible for subordinates to have the boldness to resist their superiors without fear, when in all charity they speak out in the defense of truth."* The Popes themselves teach this. **Ven. Pius IX** said: *"If a future pope teaches anything contrary to the Catholic Faith, **do not follow him**."* Even if the many should follow the Pope into heresy, and *"Even if Catholics faithful to Tradition **are reduced to a handful**, they are the ones who are the true Church of Jesus Christ,"* says St. Athanasius. **St. Robert Bellarmine, S.J.**, even wrote as follows:

> *Just as* ***it is lawful to resist the pope*** *that attacks the body, it is also lawful to resist the one who attacks souls or who disturbs civil order, or, above all, who attempts to* ***destroy the Church****. I say that* ***it is lawful to resist him by not doing what he orders and preventing his will from being executed****.*

Validly questioning or resisting a Pope is one thing, denouncing him as an antipope is altogether another. We must remember that ecclesiastical law requires that **the faithful must presume we have a valid Pope, unless the Church's highest authority formally declares otherwise with the clearest of evidence.** May the Lord continue to guide us in His truth and in faithfulness to His Church and loyalty to the Pope. At the same time, the faithful must be alert, as there are several credible prophecies, besides St. Hildegard, including some mentioned later in this book, that discuss a future false pope. God help the Church and us.

II. TWO MYSTICS FORETELL COMING CRISIS IN PAPACY

"Pray for me, that I may not flee for fear of the wolves".
Pope Benedict XVI at Inauguration Mass

1. Bl. Elizabeth Canori Mora

Bl. Elizabeth Canori Mora (d. 1825), on instructions from her confessor, wrote down revelations she received from God. Today, the manuscripts are safely kept in the archives of the Trinitarian Fathers at San Carlino, Rome. These practically unknown revelations tie in remarkably with those of the current situation of Rome and the Church today. She was beatified in 1994.

Crisis in the Church

On Christmas Eve 1813, Bl. Elizabeth was transported in ecstasy to a place refulgent with light. There she saw countless saints in adoration before a humble manger. The Infant Jesus signaled her sweetly to approach, but on drawing near she saw that He was soaking in His own Blood.

> *Just the thought of it fills me with horror. But at the same time I understood the reason for such shedding of blood was **the bad habits of many priests and religious** who do not behave according to their state in life and **the bad education given to children** by their fathers, mothers and others entrusted with this duty. They... mortally persecute Him with their bad conduct and teachings.*

Bl. Elizabeth received many other revelations concerning the devastating chaos and decadence into which Catholics, both lay and clerical, would fall. She relates that on February 24, 1814, she *"saw many ministers of the Lord who rob each other and furiously tear off the sacred vestments. I saw the sacred altars despoiled by the very ministers of God."*

Likewise, on March 22, 1814, while praying for the Holy Father she *"saw [the Pope] surrounded **by wolves** who plotted to betray him... I saw the Sanhedrin of wolves which surrounded the*

Pope, and two angels weeping...when I asked them why they were sad and lamenting, looking upon <u>Rome</u> with eyes full of compassion they responded, 'Wretched city, ungrateful people, the justice of God will chastise you.'"

On January 16, 1815, angels showed her *"many ecclesiastics who persecute Jesus Crucified and His holy Gospel under the guise of doing good...* **Like furious wolves they <u>scheme to pull the Church leader down from his throne</u>**.*"* Then she was allowed to see the terrible indignation these wolves aroused in God. *"In terror I saw the blazing* **lightening bolts** *of Divine Justice fall about me. I saw buildings collapsing in ruins. Cities, regions and the whole world fell into chaos. One heard nothing but countless weak voices calling out for mercy. Countless people will be killed."*

Concerning her vision of June 7, 1815 she wrote of *"**fierce wolves in sheep's clothing**, relentless persecutors of Jesus Crucified and His spouse the Holy Church... I saw the whole world convulsed, especially **<u>the city of Rome</u>**. How can I possibly relate what I saw of the Holy College? Because of <u>contrary doctrines</u>, together with the secular clergy, they were scattered, persecuted and murdered by the impious..."*

Justice Comes for the World

On Christmas, 1816 Bl. Elizabeth saw Our Lady, who appeared extremely sad. Upon inquiring why, Our Lady answered, *"Behold, my daughter, such great ungodliness."* Blessed Elizabeth then saw *"apostates brazenly trying to rip her most holy Son from her arms."* Confronted with such an outrage, the Mother of God ceased to only ask mercy for the world, and thus requested justice from the Eternal Father. Clothed in His inexorable Justice and full of indignation, He turned to the world, and –

*At that moment **all nature went into convulsions**, the world lost its normal order and was filled with the most terrible calamity imaginable. This will be something so deplorable and atrocious that it will reduce the world to the ultimate depths of desolation.*

On the feast of Saints Peter and Paul, June 29, 1820, she saw Saint Peter descending from heaven, robed in papal vestments and surrounded by a legion of angels. With his crosier he drew a great cross over the face of the earth, separating it into four quadrants. In each of these quadrants, he then brought forth a tree, sprouting with new life. Each tree was in the shape of a cross and enveloped in magnificent light. All the good laity and religious gathered for protection underneath these trees and were spared from the tremendous chastisement. Then, Bl. Elizabeth writes as follows:

*Woe! Woe to those unobservant religious who despise their Holy Rules. They will all perish in **the terrible chastisement** together with all who give themselves to debauchery and follow the false maxims of their deplorable contemporary philosophy!*

*...When this bloody fight will arrive, the vengeful hand of God will weigh upon these fated ones and with His omnipotence He will chastise the proud for their rashness and shameless insolence. **God will use the powers of darkness to exterminate these sectarian, iniquitous and criminal men, who plot to***

eradicate the Catholic Church, our Holy Mother, by tearing Her up by Her deepest roots, and casting Her on the ground.

God Will Laugh at Them

Bl. Elizabeth continues:

*God will laugh at their malice, and with a mere wave of His almighty right Hand, **He will punish the wicked**. The **powers of darkness** will be allowed to leave Hell and enormous crowds of devils will invade the whole world. **They will wreak great destruction and thus execute the orders of Divine Justice**, to which they are also subjected...*

God will allow wicked men to be cruelly chastised by fierce demons, because they voluntarily subjected themselves to the devil and joined in his attack of the Holy Catholic Church... They will decimate every place that idolatry was practiced to such an extent that no trace of them will remain.

The Great Restoration Begins

However, all will not end in this death and destruction. After these purifying punishments, Bl. Elizabeth saw St. Peter return on a majestic papal throne together with St. Paul, who went through the world shackling the devils and bringing them before St. Peter, who cast them back into the dark caverns from where they had come. She writes: *"Then a beautiful splendor came over the earth, to announce the reconciliation of God with mankind."*

The small flock of faithful Catholics who had taken refuge under the trees will be brought before St. Peter, who will *"choose a new pope. **All the Church will be reordered** according to the true* *dictates of the holy Gospel. The religious orders will be reestablished and the homes of Christians will become homes imbued with religion. So great will be the fervor and zeal for the glory of God that **everything will promote love of God and neighbor. The triumph, glory and honor of the Catholic Church will be established in an instant.** She will be acclaimed, venerated and esteemed by all. All will resolve to follow Her, recognizing the Vicar of Christ as the Supreme Pontiff."* She continues, saying: *"He told me many other things about this **renovation**. Many sovereigns will support the Catholic Church and be true Catholics, placing their scepters and crowns at the feet of the Holy Father and Vicar of Jesus Christ. **Many kingdoms will abandon their errors and return to the bosom of the Catholic Faith.** Entire peoples will convert, recognizing the Faith of Jesus Christ as the true religion."*

Thus will commence the universal Kingdom of the Divine Will on earth.

2. Bl. Anne Catherine Emmerich

Bl. Anne Catherine Emmerich (1774-1824) was a German Augustinian nun of great sanctity. She endured a life of sufferings, bore the stigmata of our Lord, and was a seer who witnessed scenes from the life of Christ with the vividness of one who was there. Those revelations were one of the sources used in the making of Mel Gibson's film, ***The Passion of the Christ.*** Her body is incorrupt, and she was beatified in 2004. She also foretold future occurrences in the Church. The following are from her visions pertaining to the emergence of a subversive Church of Darkness that would deceive many of the faithful.

March 22, 1820

*I saw very clearly **the errors, the aberrations, and the countless sins of men**. I saw the folly and the wickedness of their actions, against all truth and all reason. Priests were among them, and **I gladly endured my suffering** so that they may return to a better mind.*

April 12, 1820

*I had another vision of **the great tribulation**. It seems to me that **a concession** was demanded from the clergy, which could not be granted. I saw many older priests, especially one, who wept bitterly. A few younger ones were also weeping. But others, and the lukewarm among them, readily did what was demanded. It was as if people were <u>splitting into **two camps**</u>...*

Two Popes and a Counterfeit Church

May 13, 1820

*I saw also **<u>the relationship between the two popes</u>**. . .*

*I saw how baleful (harmful) would be the consequences of this **<u>false church</u>**. I saw it increase in size; heretics of every kind came into the city (of Rome). The local clergy grew lukewarm, and I saw a great darkness...*

*Once more I saw that **the Church of Peter** was undermined by a plan evolved by the secret sect (freemasonry), while storms were damaging it. But I saw also that help was coming when* *distress had reached its peak. I saw again **the Blessed Virgin ascend on the Church and spread her mantle [over it]**.*

July, 1820

***I saw the Holy Father surrounded by traitors and in great distress** about the Church. He had visions and apparitions in his hour of greatest need. I saw many good pious Bishops; but they were weak and wavering, their cowardice often got the upper hand...*

August to October, 1820

*I saw **the secret sect** relentlessly **undermining the great Church**. Near them I saw a horrible beast coming up from the sea... All over the world, good and devout people especially the clergy were harassed, oppressed and put into prison. I had the feeling that they would become martyrs...*

August 10, 1820

*I see **the Holy Father** in great anguish. He lives in a palace other than before and he admits only a limited number of friends near him. I fear that the Holy Father will suffer many more trials before he dies. I see that **the false Church of darkness is making progress** and I see the dreadful influence it has on the people...*

*I have been told to **pray much for the Church and the Pope**...The people must **pray earnestly for the extirpation (rooting out) of the dark church**. [There are many] **traitors and evildoers who were to be found among the high-ranking servants living close to [the Pope]...***

August 25, 1820

*Then I saw an apparition of **the Mother of God**, and she said that **the tribulation would be very great**. She added that people must pray fervently... They must pray above all for **the Church of Darkness** to leave Rome...*

*When **the [true] Church had been for the most part destroyed** [by the secret sect], and when only the sanctuary and altar were still standing, I saw the wreckers enter the Church with the Beast. There they met **a Woman of noble carriage who seemed to be with child** because she walked slowly (see Rev. 12). At this sight, the enemies were terrorized, and the Beast could not take but another step forward... Thereupon, I saw the Beast taking to flight towards the sea again, and the enemies were fleeing in the greatest confusion...*

September 12, 1820

*I saw **a strange church being built against every rule**... [and] **the new heterodox Church of Rome**, which seems of the same kind...*

October 1, 1820

***The Church is in great danger. We must pray so that the Pope may not leave Rome; countless evils would result if he did... there hardly remain a hundred or so priests who have not been deceived**. They all work for destruction, even the clergy...*

April 22, 1823

*I see that when **the Second Coming of Christ** approaches, **a** *bad priest will do much harm to the Church. When the time of the reign of Antichrist is near, a false religion will appear which will be opposed to the unity of God and His Church. This will cause the greatest schism the world has ever known...* *They built a large, singular, extravagant church, which was to embrace all creeds with equal rights: Evangelicals, Catholics, and all denominations, a true communion of the unholy with one shepherd and one flock. There was to be a Pope, a salaried pope, without possessions. All was made ready, many things finished; but, in place of an altar, were only abomination and desolation. Such was the new church to be, and it was for it that he had set fire to the old one; but God designed otherwise....*

Great Victory

September 10, 1820

I saw the Church of St Peter: it has been destroyed but for the Sanctuary and the main altar. St Michael came down into the Church, clad in his suit of armor, and he paused, threatening with his sword a number of unworthy pastors who wanted to enter... Then, from all over the world came priests and laymen, and they rebuilt the stone walls, since the wreckers had been unable to move the heavy foundation stones. And then I saw that the Church was being promptly rebuilt and She was more magnificent than ever before.

A false prophet of a false church in Rome, set up for the antichrist. The false prophet will dismantle the doctrine and persuade moral revision with seduction, while tearing apart the Church from within.

III. RECENT POPES WARN OF THE SIGNS OF THE TIMES

Recent Popes have spoken of the times at hand and have seen what was already beginning to occur in their lifetimes. Here are a few excerpts from them.

Pope Leo XIII

When will all these things happen? Recent prophecies have indicated that we are now in the times of the rise of evil and the earthly reign of the antichrist. Reportedly, on October 13, 1884, and on what would thirty-three years later be the date of the Miracle of Fatima, Pope Leo XIII had just completed a celebration of Mass in one of the Vatican's private chapels. Standing at the foot of the altar, he suddenly turned pale and collapsed to the floor, apparently the victim of a stroke or heart attack. However, neither malady was the cause of his collapse. Instead, he had just received a vision of the future of the Church. After a few minutes spent in what seemed like a coma, he revived and remarked to those around him, *"Oh, what a horrible picture I was permitted to see!"* During Pope Leo's ecstasy, he heard two voices, one deep and coarse, which he understood to be Satan challenging the other voice, Jesus. The conversation reportedly went like this:

Satan: *"Given enough time and enough power, I can destroy*

your Church."

Jesus: *"How much time and how much power?"*

Satan: *"100 years and a greater power over those who will give themselves to my service."*

Jesus: *"You have the time and you will have the power. Do with them what you will."*

What Leo XIII saw, as described later by those who talked to him at the time of his vision, was a period of about one hundred years when the power of Satan would reach its zenith. That period has become known as The Hundred Years' Reign of Satan. Leo XIII was so shaken by the vision of the depravity of moral and spiritual values both inside and outside the Church that he immediately composed a prayer that he then had said at the end of each Mass celebrated in the Catholic Church. The Prayer of St. Michael the Archangel was hence said continuously, until the Mass was revised in the Second Vatican Council. It is still an important part of the Rosary prayer today. We must remember that while the devil has real power granted him by God, though it is not limitless, the Lord is all-powerful and His mercy and compassion are infinite. **St. John Paul II** spoke of the continued importance of this prayer in our times, saying:

*The **Book of Revelation** refers to [the] battle, recalling before our eyes the image of St. Michael the Archangel (Revelation 12:7). Pope Leo XIII certainly had a very vivid recollection of this scene when, at the end of the [nineteenth] century, he introduced a special prayer to St. Michael throughout the Church. Although this prayer is no longer recited at the end of Mass, **I ask everyone**

not to forget [the St. Michael Prayer] *and to recite it to obtain help in the battle against forces of darkness and against the spirit of this world.*

The St. Michael Prayer

Saint Michael the Archangel,

defend us in battle;

be our protection against the wickedness and snares of the devil.

May God rebuke him, we humbly pray;

and do thou, O Prince of the heavenly host,

by the power of God,

cast into hell Satan and all the evil spirits

who prowl about the world seeking the ruin of souls.

Amen.

Ven. Pius XII

Pius XII saw the coming times. After **an apparition of Jesus and Mary**, he reportedly told one of his assistants:

*Mankind must prepare itself for sufferings such as it has never before experienced...the darkest since the deluge...The hour has struck, **the battle**, the most widespread, bitter and ferocious the world has ever known, has been joined. It must be fought to the finish... Suppose, dear friend, that **Communism** was only the most visible of the instruments of subversion to be used against the Church and the traditions of Divine Revelation ... I am worried by the Blessed Virgin's **messages to Lucy of**

*Fatima. This persistence of Mary about the dangers which menace the Church is **a divine warning against the suicide of altering the Faith, in Her liturgy** ... A day will come when the civilized world will deny its God, when **the Church will doubt** as Peter doubted. She will be tempted to believe that man has become God ... **In our churches, Christians will search in vain for the red lamp** where God awaits them, like Mary Magdalene weeping before the empty tomb, they will ask, 'Where have they taken Him?' ... I hear all around me innovators who wish to dismantle the Sacred Chapel, destroy the universal flame of the Church, reject Her ornaments and make Her feel remorse for Her historical past...*

Pope Paul VI

On October 13, 1977, the anniversary of Fatima, Paul VI stated:

*We believed that after the Council (i.e. Vatican II) would come a day of sunshine in the history of the Church. But instead there has come **a day of clouds and storms**, and of darkness of searching and uncertainties... And how did this come about?... There has been a power, an adversary power. Let us call him by his name: the devil. It is as if from some mysterious crack, no, it is not mysterious, **from some crack the smoke of Satan has entered the temple of God**. (1972)*

The tail of the devil is functioning in the disintegration of the Catholic World. The darkness of Satan has entered and spread throughout the Catholic Church even to its summit.

Apostasy, the loss of the faith, is spreading throughout the world and into the highest levels within the Church.

St. John Paul II

Pope John Paul II, as Karol Cardinal Wojtyla, spoke these words during a visit to the United States in 1976:

> We are now standing in the face of **the greatest historical confrontation** humanity has gone through. I do not think that wide circles of the American society or wide circles of the Christian community realize this fully. We are now facing **the final confrontation** between the Church and the anti-Church, of the Gospel versus the anti-Gospel. This confrontation lies within the plans of Divine Providence... It is a test of 2,000 years of culture and Christian civilization with all of its consequences for human dignity, individual rights, human rights and the rights of nations.

By this statement, he makes it clear he had a sense of the times and wanted to warn us about them.

Pope Benedict XVI

In 2008, Pope Benedict spoke of the end times, saying:

> Before the Lord's arrival, there will be **apostasy**, and one well described as the 'man of lawlessness', 'the son of perdition' must be revealed, who tradition would come to call **the Antichrist**.

As Cardinal Joseph Ratzinger (Pope Benedict XVI), he wrote an article, *"The Church Will Become Small"*, saying:

The Church will become small and *will have to start afresh more or less from the beginning...*

And so it seems certain to me that the Church is facing very hard times. **The real crisis has scarcely begun.** *We will have to count on* **terrific upheavals**. *But I am equally certain about what will remain at the end: not the Church of the political cult, which is dead already, but* **the Church of faith***. She may well no longer be the dominant social power to the extent that she was until recently; but she will enjoy* **a fresh blossoming** *and be seen as man's home, where he will find life and hope beyond death.*

Benedict XVI has also related our times to the Book of Revelation, saying:

The threat of judgment also concerns us, *the Church in Europe, Europe and the West in general... the Lord is also crying out to our ears the words that* **in the Book of Revelation** *he addresses to the Church of Ephesus: 'If you do not repent I will come to you and remove your lampstand from its place'... let this warning ring out with its full seriousness in our hearts, while crying to the Lord: 'Help us to repent! Give all of us the grace of true renewal! Do not allow your light in our midst to blow out! Strengthen our faith, our hope and our love, so that we can bear good fruit.'*

We see of course that today too the dragon wants to devour God *who made himself a Child. Do not fear for this seemingly frail God;* **the fight has already been won***... We see this power,* *the force of **the red dragon**... in new and different ways. It exists in the form of materialistic ideologies that tell us **it is absurd to think of God; it is absurd to observe God's commandments**: they are a leftover from a time past. Life is only worth living for its own sake. Take everything we can get in this brief moment of life. **Consumerism, selfishness, and entertainment alone** are worthwhile.*

Pope Benedict warned about this erosion of truth, when just before being elected Pope, he discussed the perils of our times – that of the prevailing culture today which has but one message of promoting relativism, whereby each person today is directed to be *"tossed here and there, carried about by every wind of doctrine"*. In trepidation, he declared: *"We are building **a dictatorship of relativism** that does not recognize anything as definitive and whose ultimate goal consists solely of one's own ego and desires."* And consequences will be dire.

In late 2010, Benedict went on to prophetically draw a link between the fall of the Roman Empire and our own times. First, describing the decline of the Roman Empire he said, *"The disintegration of the key principles of law and of the fundamental moral attitudes underpinning them burst open the dams which until that time had protected peaceful coexistence among peoples... There was no power in sight that could put a stop to this decline."* Then, comparing those times to our own, he added: *"For all its new hopes and possibilities, our world is at the same time troubled by the sense that **moral consensus is collapsing**, consensus without which juridical and political structures cannot function. Consequently the forces*

mobilized for the defense of such structures seem doomed to failure."
Referring to these recent *"**great tribulations** to which we have been exposed"*, he concluded: ***"The very future of the world is at stake."***

During his pontificate, Benedict hinted about his own retirement (and possible future fate). On April 29, 2009, he visited the tomb of an obscure medieval Pope named **St. Celestine V**. After a brief prayer, Benedict left his pallium, the symbol of his office as Bishop of Rome and Pope, on Celestine's tomb. Later, on July 4, 2010, Pope Benedict again went to visit St. Celestine, this time at the cathedral where his relics are entombed. Few people noticed his actions at the time. But, as he himself retired in 2013, his gestures took on a significant and personal meaning. And it relates to St. Celestine, who had been elevated to the papacy, somewhat against his will, shortly before his 80th birthday (Ratzinger was 78 when he was elected Pope in 2005). Just five months later, after issuing a formal decree allowing popes to resign, Pope Celestine V abruptly resigned from the papacy.

And now Pope Benedict XVI has chosen to follow in the footsteps of this venerable model. It might be interesting to note that after retiring, Pope Celestine's successor, Pope Boniface VIII had him imprisoned in a suffocating cell, where he died 10 months later. Some have even considered that he may have been directly murdered, as a hole was later found in his skull (but this theory has been somewhat dispelled).

We may wonder what the fate will be for Benedict, who is now Pope Emeritus. There is an interesting prophecy of **St. Pius X**, who early in the twentieth century revealed some detail about a future retired pope, saying:

> *I saw one of my successors taking to flight over the bodies of his brethren. He will take refuge in disguise somewhere; and after a short retirement he will die a cruel death.*

Time will tell. We must pray for our Church and Pope(s) in these times. What great insights and words of caution these recent Popes give us for our times!

IV. PROPHECIES OF SAINTS ON THE LATTER TIMES

There are other prophecies of saints that discuss the latter times, the Pope, and the eventual outcome. Here are a few examples:

St. Francis of Assisi reportedly gave a papal prophecy that seems to align with those of the three mystics previously discussed: St. Hildegard, Bl. Elizabeth Mora and Bl. Anne Catherine Emmerich. Shortly before he died, St. Francis called together his followers and warned them of the end-time troubles, saying:

> *1. The time is fast approaching in which there will be great trials and afflictions;* **perplexities and dissensions,** *both spiritual and temporal, will abound; the charity of many will grow cold, and the malice of the wicked will increase.*
>
> *2. The devils will have unusual power... there will be very few Christians who will obey the true Sovereign Pontiff and the Roman Church with loyal hearts and perfect charity. At the time of this tribulation* **a man, not (authentically) canonically**

elected, will be raised to the Pontificate, *who, by his cunning, will endeavor to draw many into error and death.*

3. ... Many will consent to error instead of opposing it.

*4. There will be **such diversity of opinions and schisms** among the people, the religious and the clergy, that, except those days were shortened, according to the words of the Gospel, even the elect would be led into error, were they not specially guided, amid such great confusion, by the immense mercy of God.*

*5. Those who are found **faithful will receive the crown of life**...*

*6. Those who **preserve their fervor and adhere to virtue with love and zeal for the truth**, **will suffer injuries and, persecutions as rebels and schismatics**; for their persecutors, urged on by the evil spirits, will say they are rendering a great service to God by destroying such pestilent men from the face of the earth. But the Lord will be the refuge of the afflicted, and will save all who trust in Him... and they will prefer to perish rather than consent to falsehood and perfidy.*

*7. Some preachers will keep silence about the truth, and others will trample it under foot and deny it. Sanctity of life will be held in derision even by those who outwardly profess it, for in those days **Jesus Christ will send them not a true Pastor, but a destroyer**.*" (From *Works of the Seraphic Father St. Francis of Assisi*, R. Washbourne, London, 1882, 248-250. Though coming from a solid source, two recent articles – Don Francesco Ricossa in Sodalitium, April 1999, and Frere Jean O.F.M.Cap. in "Le Sel de la terre", Spring 1999 – question whether Francis really said this prophecy. Still, it remains plausible and nevertheless intriguing.)

Visionary **Bl. Anna Maria Taigi**, whose body is incorrupt, prophesied about the coming universal revolution and scourge, saying:

*God will send... **wars, revolutions and other evils**... **Religion shall be persecuted**, and priests massacred. **Churches shall be closed**, but only for a short time. **The Holy Father will be obliged to leave Rome.***

Brother **John of the Cleft Rock** (14th Century), a renowned mystic, reported about our times, saying:

*Towards the **end of the world**, tyrants and hostile mobs will **rob the Church** and the clergy of all their possessions and will **afflict** and martyr them. Those who heap the most abuse upon them will be held in high esteem. **At that time, the Pope with his cardinals will have to flee Rome** in tragic circumstances to a place where they will be unknown. **The Pope will die a cruel death in his exile.** The sufferings of the Church will be much greater than at any previous time in her history.*

*But **God will raise a holy Pope**, and the Angels will rejoice. Enlightened by God, this man will rebuild almost the whole world through his holiness. **He will lead everyone to the true Faith**. Everywhere, the fear of God, virtue, and good morals will prevail. He will lead all erring sheep back to the fold, and there shall be one faith, one law, one rule of life, and one baptism on earth. All men will love each other and do good, and all quarrels and wars will cease.*

St. Alphonsus Liguori, Doctor of the Church, prophetically stated:

The devil has always attempted, by means of the heretics, to **deprive the world of the Mass**, making them precursors of the Anti-Christ, who, before anything else, will try to abolish and **will actually abolish the Holy Sacrament** of the altar, as a punishment for the sins of men, according to the prediction of Daniel 'And strength was given him against the continual sacrifice' (Daniel 8:12).

St. Nicholas von Flue also prophetically wrote:

The Church will be punished because the majority of Her members, high and low, will become so perverted. The Church will sink deeper and deeper until She will at last seem to be extinguished, and the succession of Peter and the other Apostles to have expired. But, after this, **She will be victoriously exalted** in the sight of all doubters.

Ven. Fulton Sheen, in his book, *Communism and the Conscience of the West*, insightfully discusses the coming Antichrist and what he will be like, saying:

The Antichrist will <u>not</u> be so called; otherwise he would have no followers. [The devil is] described as an angel fallen from heaven, as 'the Prince of this world,' **whose business it is to tell us that there is no other world**. His logic is simple: if there is no heaven there is no hell; if there is no hell, then there is no sin; if there is no sin, then there is no judge, and if there is no judgment then evil is good and good is evil. But above all these descriptions, **Our Lord tells us that [the Antichrist] will be so much like Himself that he would deceive even the elect** – and certainly no devil ever *seen in picture books could deceive even the elect. How will he come in this new age to win followers to his religion?*

*The pre-Communist Russian belief is that he will come disguised as **the Great Humanitarian**; he will talk peace, prosperity and plenty not as means to lead us to God, but as ends in themselves... [He will lead humanity] to have a new religion without a Cross, a liturgy without a world to come, a religion to destroy a religion, or a politics which is a religion – one that renders unto Caesar even the things that are God's.*

*In the midst of all his seeming love for humanity and his glib talk of freedom and equality, he will have one great secret which he will tell to no one: he will not believe in God. Because his religion will be brotherhood without the fatherhood of God, he will deceive even the elect. **He will set up a counterchurch which will be the ape of the Church**, because he, [as the tool of] the Devil, is the ape of God. It will have all the notes and characteristics of the Church, but in reverse and emptied of its divine content. It will be **a mystical body of the Antichrist** that will in all externals resemble the mystical body of Christ... Then will be verified a paradox – the very objections with which men in the last century rejected the Church will be the reasons why they will now accept the counterchurch (it will claim to be infallible when its visible head speaks definitively).*

What Are We To Do?

Our Lady of Good Success gives some good advice to Ven. Mariana de Jesus Torres about these times and how we should respond, saying:

> Therefore, **clamor insistently without tiring and weep with bitter tears** in the privacy of your heart, imploring our Celestial Father that, for love of the Eucharistic Heart of my Most Holy Son and His Precious Blood shed with such generosity and the profound bitterness and sufferings of His cruel Passion and Death, He might take pity on His ministers and bring to an end those Ominous times, **sending to His Church the Prelate** who will restore the spirit of its priests.

St. Margaret Mary Alacoque reminds us that in these times we have a final hope in the Sacred Heart of Jesus:

> I understand that the **devotion to the Sacred Heart** is the last effort of His Love during the latter times.

Jesus is also sending His Mother from Heaven to console us. Almost 500 years ago, **Our Lady of Guadalupe** came to the Aztecs of the New World to give them a great Miracle, which opened them to conversion and faith. Just as the Aztecs were engaged in human sacrifice and Satanism, so too, today the whole world is engaging in the human sacrifice of the unborn through abortion. Our world has handed itself over to the reign of Satan (remember Leo XIII's vision of the **100 Year's Reign of Satan**) through the onslaught of unrepented personal and social sins of our times, worshipping self, money, and pleasure (see 2 Timothy 3:1-5). And just as God did with the Aztecs, we await God's intervention again today with the global Warning (colliding comet and illumination of conscience) and new Great Miracle. What a great day that will be! But, alas, even then some will still not listen; and so God's Gift of Divine Mercy and Great Miracle will be followed afterwards by His justice and divine chastisement.

In all this to come, we have nothing to fear, as Our Lady told St. Juan Diego, and which she gently whispers to us today, saying:

Know and understand well…

*I am the ever-Virgin Holy Mary, Mother of the True God for whom we live, of the Creator of all things, Lord of heaven and the earth… [I wish to] give **all my love, compassion, help, and protection**, because I am your merciful Mother, **to you…** and all the rest who love me, invoke and confide in me; [I promise to listen] to their lamentations, and remedy all their miseries, afflictions and sorrows… Hear me and understand well…*

*Let nothing frighten or grieve you. **Let not your heart be disturbed.** Do not fear any other sickness or anguish.*

***Am I not here, who is your Mother?** Are you not under my protection? Am I not your health? Are you not happily within my fold? What else do you wish?*

Do not grieve nor be disturbed by anything.

What a wonderful heavenly Mother we have! What consolation! We have nothing to fear or worry about when we call upon our spiritual Mother in prayer. And when we do, everything will work out for the good! Let us reflect upon these words of Our Mother often, words she is addressing to each of us today. Amen!

CHAPTER 3

Jesus Is Revealing the Way of Peace Today – Through the Heavenly Messages of Our Times

God's temple in heaven was opened,
*and **the Ark** of his covenant could be seen in the temple...*
*A **great sign** appeared in the sky,*
*a **Woman** (Mary) clothed with the **sun**,*
*with the **moon** under her feet,*
*and on her head a crown of twelve **stars**.*
Revelation 11:19f

The power of Mary over all devils
will be particularly outstanding in the last period of time.
She will extend the Kingdom of Christ over all idolaters and Muslims,
*and there will **be a glorious period***
***when Mary is ruler and Queen of Hearts**.*
St. Louis de Montfort

I was already convinced that Mary
leads us to Jesus, her Son.
*Now I am convinced that **in this time***
***Jesus leads us also to Mary**, His mother.*
John Paul II

Many heavenly prophecies have been given to us from Heaven, becoming themselves *"signs of the times"*, and leading us up to the unfolding of the great battle, which will prepare the world for the new

Kingdom of the Divine Will.

I. APPROVED MARIAN PROPHECIES ABOUT OUR TIMES

We will now review some of these recognized and approved apparitions of Mary about our times.

Our Lady of Good Success

The Church-recognized apparitions of Our Lady of Good Success (1611) to the incorrupt Ven. Mother Mariana of Quito (Ecuador) gave five *"meanings"* concerning the sanctuary light that Our Lady says will go out in the Church during the great battle:

First Meaning: First, from the end of the Nineteenth Century through the Twentieth Century, various heresies will flourish and the light of faith will go out in souls because of almost total moral corruption.

Second Meaning: Then, many priests will become corrupted and the good priests will be ridiculed, oppressed and despised; religious communities will be abandoned and many true vocations will be lost for lack of prudent and skillful direction to form them.

Third Meaning: There will arise a spirit of impurity, which will flood the public places like a deluge of filth. The licentiousness will be such that there will be almost no more virgin souls in the world. Innocence will almost no longer be found in children, nor modesty in women.

Fourth Meaning: The sects will penetrate into the hearts of families and destroy even the children. There will be unbridled luxury which, acting thus to ensnare the rest of us into sin, will conquer innumerable frivolous souls who will be lost.

Then, the Church will go through a dark night for lack of a Pope to watch over it.

Satan will then take control of the earth through faithless men. There will be all sorts of chastisements: plagues, famines, war, apostasy, and the loss of souls. There will be a terrible war and it will seem as though wickedness will triumph.

Fifth Meaning: During the supreme moment of need, men possessing great wealth will look on with indifference while the Church is oppressed, virtue is persecuted, and evil triumphs. They will not use their wealth to fight evil or to reconstruct the Faith. The people will be swept away by all vices and passions.

But, then will come the time of Our Lady and her Son. In astounding fashion, she will destroy Satan's pride, casting him beneath her feet, assisting her Son in chaining him up in the depths of hell, leaving the Church freed from his cruel tyranny – so reveals the approved messages of Our Lady of Good Success. How can it be more clear?!

Our Lady of the Miraculous Medal and the Two Hearts

In 1830, the Blessed Mother appeared in a vision to **St. Catherine Labouré**, whose body is incorrupt in Rue du Bac, Paris. The Blessed Virgin announced the forthcoming End-Days battle with the Devil, as symbolized in the *"Miraculous Medal"*. Mary asked her to have a medal made of the vision, which showed Mary standing on a globe of the world, with the serpent (Satan) crushed beneath her feet, with rays of light (grace) coming forth from her hands, encircled by the words: *"O Mary, conceived without sin, pray for us who have recourse to you."* On the back of the medal, there is an *"M"* and a Cross, with **the Two Hearts** of Jesus and Mary, all encircled by twelve stars. Mary promised: *"All who wear it will receive great graces."* This medal quickly became known as the Miraculous Medal. This apparition in 1830 was the first indication from Heaven to the world that **God wants us to unite with the Two Hearts** of Jesus and Mary together to assure victory in the battle of the end times. **The stars** about Our Lady's head indicate **those who consecrate themselves to her Immaculate Heart (and to the Sacred Heart)**, who form part of her victorious army, and who allow themselves to be guided by her in order to fight this battle and to attain in the end the greatest victory. Through this medal, the period of **the Age of Mary** begins and the final battle is pre-announced. In 1987, Our Lady said through mystic **Maria Esperanza**: ***"Do not stop wearing My miraculous medal** to cover yourselves, in order to be protected... also **distribute it generously** so sinners may be converted, the sick may be healed, and the moral values of **today's world may be reestablished!**"*

La Salette

In 2002, Mariologist Fr. Rene Laurentin received the imprimatur for his book on the apocalyptic messages and prophecies concerning the Church-approved apparitions of La Salette. In the 1851 version of the secret of La Salette, Melanie spoke about the Antichrist, saying:

> *Lastly,* **hell will reign** *on earth. It will be then that the* **Antichrist** *will [come]. The seasons will be changed, the earth will produce only bad fruits… there will be horrible earthquakes which will cause to be engulfed mountains, cities…*
>
> **<u>Rome will lose the faith and become the seat of the antichrist</u>…** **The Church will be <u>eclipsed</u>,** *the world will be in consternation. Woe to the inhabitants of the earth! There will be* **bloody wars and famines;** *pestilences and contagious diseases… thunders which will shake cities, earthquakes which will engulf countries… Who will be able to overcome, if God does not shorten the time of the ordeal?*
>
> **By the blood, the tears and the prayers of the just,** *God will let Himself be swayed, Enoch and Elijah will be put to death; pagan Rome will disappear; fire from Heaven will fall and will consume three cities; all the universe will be struck with terror… faith alone will live. Behold the time; the abyss opens. Behold the king of kings of darkness.* **Behold the beast** *with his subjects, calling himself the savior of the world.*

Abbé Combe, the editor of the 1904 edition of the secret, adds the following note after this paragraph:

> I understand from Melanie (the visionary) that the Church will be "*eclipsed*" in this two-fold sense: *1) that* **<u>one will not know which is the true Pope</u>**; *2) for a time:* **<u>the holy Sacrifice will cease to be offered (validly) in churches</u>**, *and also in houses – so there will be no more (valid) public worship. But she saw that yet*

the holy Sacrifice would not cease: it would be offered in caves,
in tunnels, in barns and in alcoves.

Just as Scripture foretold: *"In the end time... the daily sacrifice [will be]*
abolished and the desolating abomination [will be] set up" (Daniel
12:11). No valid Eucharist celebrated! We will not know which is the true
Pope! La Salette confirms, as Our Lady of Good Success similarly
warned, along with several saints including St. Hildegard, Bl. Mora, Bl.
Emmerich, and St. Francis, that a false pope, the false prophet, will come.

Our Lady of Fatima and Today

Our Lady of Fatima asked for all God's faithful to enter into
her Immaculate Heart, saying: *"God wishes to establish throughout*
*the world devotion to **my Immaculate Heart**."*

A Special Request from Heaven: Our Lady of Fatima requested
the Consecration of Russia to her Immaculate Heart. She said it would
be done, but not until very late. Our Lady of Fatima said:

> ***If** people do as I shall ask many souls will be saved, and there*
> *will be peace.... **But if** people do not cease offending God...*
> *war, famine, persecution of the Church and of the Holy Father.*
> *To prevent this, I shall come to ask the **consecration of Russia***
> ***to my Immaculate Heart and Communions of reparation on***
> ***the first Saturdays.** If my requests are heard, Russia will be*
> *converted and there will be peace. If not, she will spread her*
> *errors throughout the world, fomenting wars and persecution*
> *of the Church. The good will suffer martyrdom; the Holy*
> *Father will suffer much; different nations will be annihilated.*

*But __in the end__ my Immaculate Heart will triumph. The Holy Father **will consecrate Russia** to me, which will be converted, and some time of peace will be granted to humanity.*

Even though John Paul II made a consecration of the world with the Bishops in 1984 that produced some wonderful fruits (fall of Berlin Wall and initial fall of Cold War Communism), it seems Russia will still be converted in the near future during the Second Pentecost, as Our Lady promised would occur only *"in the end."* So, the prophecy that Russia will be converted is guaranteed. However, this guarantee doesn't seem to guarantee whether or not Russia will cause much havoc and will thus be the receiver of God's just anger. Prophecy seems to indicate it will be as such, though this is of course conditional. And what of those First Saturday Communions of reparation? How often have you fulfilled this heavenly request? See more on how to do this in the last chapter of this book.

At a Mass on May 13, 2010 at the Fatima Shrine, Pope Benedict said that it would be *"mistaken"* to consider the prophetic mission of the apparitions at Fatima complete. He said, **"We would be mistaken to think that the prophetic mission of Fatima is complete."** *"Mankind,"* the Pope noted, *"has succeeded in unleashing a cycle of death and terror, but failed in bringing it to an end."* **Looking to us today**, he said that in Scripture, *"we often find that God seeks righteous men and women in order **to save the city of man**."* Benedict recalled when Mary asked the visionaries of Fatima, *"Do you want to offer yourselves to God, to endure all the sufferings which He will send you, in an act of reparation for the sins by which He is offended* *and of supplication for the conversion of sinners?"*, while alluding that she was asking the same question to us today more than ever. Looking to 2017, Benedict prophetically concluded with the prayer: *"May the seven years which separate us from the centenary of the apparitions* **hasten the fulfillment of the prophecy of the triumph of the Immaculate Heart of Mary**, *to the glory of the Most Holy Trinity."*

Is there more to the Fatima secret not yet revealed? Well, before he later revealed the content of the 3rd Secret of Fatima in 2000, John Paul II spoke to a select group of German Catholics at Fulda during his 1980 visit to Germany. Here is an excerpt from his words:

The Holy Father was asked, *"What about the Third Secret of Fatima? Should it not have already been published by 1960?"*

Pope John Paul II replied: *"Given the seriousness of the contents, my predecessors in the Petrine office diplomatically preferred to postpone publication* **so as not to encourage the world power of Communism to make certain moves.**

*On the other hand, it should be sufficient for all Christians to know this: if there is **a message** in which it is written that the oceans will flood whole areas of the earth, and that from one moment to the next millions of people will perish, truly the publication of such a message is no longer something to be so much desired."*

At this point the Pope grasped a Rosary and said: ***"Here is the remedy against this evil. Pray, pray, and ask for nothing more. Leave everything else to the Mother of God."***

The Holy Father was then asked: *"What is going to happen to the Church?"*

He answered: *"**We must prepare ourselves to suffer great trials before long**, such as will demand of us a disposition to give up even life, and a total dedication to Christ and for Christ. With your and my prayer **it is possible to mitigate this tribulation, but it is no longer possible to avert it**, because **only thus can the Church be effectively renewed**. How many times has the renewal of the Church sprung from blood! This time, too, it will not be otherwise. **We must be strong and prepared, and trust in Christ and His Mother, and be very, very assiduous in praying the Rosary."**

In his book, *The Last Secret of Fatima*, Cardinal Bertone, (now former) Vatican Secretary of State, acknowledged that John Paul II did in fact say these words (p. 48). What clarity, for those who can see!

The Third Secret of Fatima, given by Our Lady, was revealed publically by John Paul II in 2000 (the first two secrets having already been revealed), and reveals more heavenly prophecy about the sufferings of a pope and the faithful in these times, as follows:

*At the left of Our Lady and a little above, we saw **an Angel with a flaming sword** in his left hand; flashing, it gave out flames that looked as though they would set the world on fire; but they died out in contact with **the splendor that Our Lady radiated** towards him from her right hand: pointing to the earth with his right hand, the Angel cried out in a loud voice: 'Penance, Penance, Penance!' And we saw in an immense light that is God: 'something similar to how people appear in a mirror when they pass in front of it' a Bishop dressed in White 'we had the impression that it was the Holy Father'. Other Bishops, Priests, men and women Religious* *going up a steep mountain, at the top of which there was a big Cross of rough-hewn trunks as of a cork-tree with the bark; before reaching there the Holy Father passed through a big **city half in ruins** and half trembling with halting step, afflicted with pain and sorrow, he prayed for the souls of **the corpses** he met on his way; having reached the top of the mountain, on his knees at the foot of the big Cross [**the pope] was killed** by a group of soldiers who fired bullets and arrows at him, and in the same way there died one after another the other Bishops, Priests, men and women Religious, and various lay people of different ranks and positions. Beneath the two arms of the Cross, there were two Angels each with a crystal aspersorium in his hand, in which they gathered up **the blood of the Martyrs** and with it sprinkled the souls that were making their way to God.*

Cardinal Ratzinger spoke about the conditional nature of this prophecy when he said, *"The vision speaks of dangers and how we might be saved from them."* This vision in many ways matches the famous vision of St. John Bosco, which both speak of the martyrdom of a pope and the final ultimate victory. Let us follow the true Pope, with the authentic Magisterium, through the ruined city of this world today, over the dead corpses (those living in mortal sin), and move forward to the hill of Calvary and Victory. And let us – *"Be not afraid!"*

St. Faustina, Our Lady's Prophecy, and the 'Great Sign' of Mercy

Jesus, I trust in You.
O Sacred Heart of Jesus, I place all my trust in You.
O Blood and Water, which gushed forth from the

Heart of Jesus as a fount of Mercy for us, I trust in You.

St. Faustina, the twentieth century Polish nun who became the Lord's Apostle of Mercy, received many private revelations from Jesus and Mary, especially concerning the Devotion to His Sacred Heart, the Fount of Mercy. Jesus asked for her to share His great desire to give humanity His mercy, which comes to us in several ways in these latter times. Jesus revealed to her the divine decree for the Feast of Divine Mercy, which the Church has approved for the Second Sunday of Easter. He also expressed His desire to be venerated through the Image of His Sacred Heart, which is the Image of Divine Mercy, saying: *"I promise that the soul that will venerate this image* **will not perish**. *I also promise* **victory over its enemies** *already here on earth, especially at the hour of death. I myself will defend it as My own glory... By means of this image I shall grant* **many graces** *to souls. It is to be a reminder of the demands of My mercy, because even the strongest faith is of no avail without works."* Jesus asks us to imitate Him in being merciful – in deeds, words, and prayer.

The Perfect Devotion centered on the Heart of Christ is a final gift of Christ's love for humanity in these evil times, as St. Margaret Mary confirms: ***"This devotion (of His Sacred Heart is) the last effort of His love that He will grant to men in these latter ages, in order to withdraw them from the empire of Satan*** *which He desires to destroy."* God has waited until our times to draw our special attention to His Heart because He wants His Heart to be the remedy of our souls in these times, to rouse us from our lethargy so that we will become inflamed with Divine Love and seek consolation in His Most Compassionate Heart. God is asking our help in the destruction of *Satan's empire*! And it is through sacrifice and mercy that Satan will be defeated, and then will come justice. Jesus said to St. Faustina:

> *You will prepare the world* ***for My final coming.***
> *Speak to the world about My mercy...* ***It is a sign for***
> ***the end times.*** *After it will come the Day of Justice.*

St. Faustina writes about a vision she received showing her how powerful the Chaplet of Divine Mercy prayer is for saving sinners: *"I saw a great light, with God the Father in the midst of it. Between this light and the earth I saw Jesus nailed to the Cross, and in such a way that God, wanting to look upon the earth, had to look through Our Lord's wounds and I understood that God blessed the earth for the sake of Jesus...* ***I saw an Angel, the executor of God's wrath... about to strike the earth...*** *I began to beg God earnestly for the world with words which I heard interiorly (the Chaplet of Divine Mercy). As I prayed in this way, I saw the Angel's helplessness, and he could not carry out the just punishment."* As with the Third Secret of Fatima, this prophetic vision concerns the coming of God's just wrath for the sins of humanity, of Our Lady's intervention, and the heavenly calling for victim souls to offer sacrifices and reparation for sinners. What a motivation this is to us!

In addition to these words of Our Lord, **the Mother of Mercy, the Blessed Virgin**, gave to Faustina this prophecy and instruction:

> *You have to speak to the world about His great mercy and* ***prepare the world for the Second Coming*** *of Him who will come, not as a merciful Savior, but* ***as a just Judge.*** *Oh how*

*terrible is that day! Determined is the day of justice, the day of divine wrath. The angels tremble before it. Speak to souls about this great mercy **while it is still the time** for granting mercy.*

To St. Faustina, Our Lord stated, *"I am **prolonging the time of mercy** for the sake of [sinners],"* while warning, *"But woe to them if they do not recognize this time of My visitation."* So, let us cry for *souls*!

St. Faustina received a prophecy from the Lord about the end times, about a coming event for the whole world – a divine Warning of Mercy. Jesus spoke to St. Faustina about a great darkness and **a Great Sign of the Cross**, explaining what would accompany it, saying:

> ***Before I come as a just judge, I am coming first as 'King of Mercy!'*** *Let all men now approach the throne of my mercy with absolute confidence! Some time before the last days of final justice arrive, there will be given to mankind a **great sign in the heavens** of this sort: all the light of the heavens will be totally extinguished... There will be **a great darkness** over the whole earth. Then **a great sign of the cross will appear** in the sky. From the openings from where the hands and feet of the savior were nailed will come forth great lights which will light up the earth for a period of time. This will happen before the very final days. It is **the sign for the end of the world. After it will come the days of justice!** Let souls have recourse to the fount of my mercy while there is still time! Woe to him who does not recognize the time of my visitation...*

In the Old Covenant I sent prophets wielding thunderbolts to My people. **Today I am sending you with My mercy to the people of the whole world.** *I do not want to punish aching mankind, but I desire to heal it, pressing it to My merciful Heart. I use punishment when they themselves force Me to do so; My hand is reluctant to take hold of the sword of justice.* **Before the Day of Justice, I am sending the Day of Mercy.**

This prophecy of the coming divine Warning of the *"Great Sign of the Cross"* in the sky is supported by Christ in Scripture, when He says:

Immediately after the distress of those days
the **sun will be darkened**, *the moon will not give its light, the stars will*
fall from the sky and the powers of the heavens will be shaken.
And then **the sign of the Son of man** *will appear in heaven;*
then, too, all the peoples of the earth will beat their breasts;
and they will see the Son of man coming
on the clouds of heaven with power and great glory.
Matthew 24:30

Apparitions of Heede

In the Church-recognized apparitions of Heede, Our Lady appeared to four girls at Heede, a small village in northern Germany in 1937. Jesus Himself also appeared, delivering an apocalyptic message to one of the girls, Greta Gansforth, as follows:

Men did not listen to My Most Holy Mother when She appeared to them at Fatima and admonished them to do penance. **Now I Myself am coming at the last hour** *to warn and admonish mankind!* **The times are very serious!** *Men should at last do penance, turn away from their sins and pray, pray much* **in order** *that the wrath of God may be mitigated!* Particularly the Holy Rosary should be prayed very often! *The Rosary is very powerful with God! Worldly pleasures and amusements should be restricted*...

Mankind is worse than before the deluge. Mankind is suffocating in sin. Hatred and greed rule their hearts. This is *the work of the Devil.* They live in great darkness...

Mercy will again gain victory over justice. *My faithful souls* should not be asleep now like the disciples on Mt. Olivet. They should pray without ceasing and gain all they can for themselves and for others.

Tremendous things are in preparation; it will be *terrible as never before since the foundation of the world.* All those who in these grave times have suffered so much are martyrs and form the seed for the new Church...

The Blessed Virgin Mary and all the choirs of Angels will be active during the happenings. Hell believes that it is sure of the harvest, but I will snatch it away from them.

I will come with My *peace. With a few faithful, I will build up My Kingdom.* As a flash of lightening *this Kingdom will come*... much faster than mankind will realize. I will give them *a special light...* Pray without ceasing!

This New Kingdom will indeed come, quickly and soon! May it be so!

Our Lady of All Nations

Our Lady appeared in Amsterdam in the Church-approved (by

Bishop Jozef Marianus Punt of Haarlem on May 31, 2002) apparitions of Our Lady of All Nations and asked for the Church to declare a final Marian dogma. Our Lady prophesied about the fifth and final dogma of Mary that will bring a period of peace to the world and to humanity. To visionary Ida Peerdeman on May 31, 1954, Our Lady said:

> *The Lady of All Nations wishes for unity in the true Holy Spirit.* ***The world is covered by a false spirit, by Satan.*** *Once the dogma, the final dogma in Marian history, has been proclaimed, the Lady of All Nations will grant peace,* ***true peace****, to the world. The nations, however, must pray my prayer, together with the Church. They shall know that the Lady of All Nations has come as* **Coredemptrix, Mediatrix and Advocate***.*

And twenty-five years later, to the day, Our Lord promised through visionary, Ida: *"The Holy Father will proclaim her Co-redemptrix, Mediatrix and Advocate."* She says to us today: *"To you all, however, falls the task of introducing the Lady of All Nations to the whole world... Do **fight and ask for this Dogma**, it is the Crowning of your Lady!"*

Our Lady of All Nations prophesied about **warning signs** to come as indication of the apocalyptic time, including meteors and natural disasters, along with political conflicts and economic disasters. Our Lady promises the nations of the world a new spring of *"grace, redemption, and peace"* that will save the world from *"degeneration, disaster, and war"*. Do you understand? She promised that if we seek her help, she would bestow **Grace, Redemption, and Peace** to stave off **degeneration, disaster, and war**. What a great hope we should place in Mary. She is our hope!

The Our Lady of Akita statue (which is of Our Lady of All Nations) wept 101 times. In the end, Our Lady of Akita said: *"Whoever entrusts themselves to me will be saved."* What more do *you* need? Respond now, Our Lady is pleading!

A New Prayer to Save the World

A special Prayer of Our Lady of All Nations was also given through this apparition, so *"that under this title and through this prayer,* ***she may deliver the world from a great world catastrophe...*** ***Through this prayer the Lady shall save the world."*** After giving this special prayer for the world, Our Lady said to Ida about The Lady of All Nations Prayer:

> *You do not know how great and how important this prayer is before God! You cannot estimate the great value this will have. You do not know what the future has in store... It is given in order to call down the True Spirit upon the world...* ***This prayer has been given for the conversion of the world.***
>
> *I am the Lady of All Peoples... 'Who once was Mary.' Here is the meaning of this formula: Mary was known as Mary by a great number of men, but now,* ***in the new era which is opening, I wish to be known as the Lady of All Peoples.*** *And everyone will understand that.*

Mary is not relinquishing her name, but publicly expanding her office and heavenly role (Revelation 12) for the conversion and salvation of all souls. We need to respond, as she has requested, and pray and spread her powerful prayer, which is as follows:

The Lady of All Nations Prayer

Lord Jesus Christ, Son of the Father,
send now Your Spirit over the earth.
Let the Holy Spirit live in the hearts of all nations,
that they may be preserved
from degeneration, disaster and war.
May the Lady of All Nations,
who once was Mary,
be our Advocate. Amen.

Mediatrix of All Grace (Marienfried)

There is another Marian apparition that speaks of Mary's role as Mediatrix, as she did as Our Lady of All Nations. The Blessed Virgin Mary appeared to Barbara Reuss three times in 1946. The local Bishop has affirmed this apparition for faith expression. On March 20, 2000, the Bishop of Augsburg, Germany, declared that the faithful may make pilgrimages to the shrine.

First Vision: April 25, 1946

The Blessed Mother said to Barbara:

> *Where the strongest confidence reigns and where it is taught to men that I can do everything, there **I will spread peace**... I print my sign on the forehead of my children. The star (Satan) will pursue my sign, but my sign will prevail over the star.*

Second Vision: May 25, 1946

*I am the powerful **Mediatrix of Graces**... you only find favor with the Son through my intercession... It is true that the world* *was consecrated to my Immaculate Heart, but... I demand that the world **live this consecration**.*

Have unreserved confidence in my Immaculate Heart! *Believe that I am able to do everything with my Son...*

*The world will have to drain the cup of wrath to the dregs because of the countless sins through which His Heart is offended. The Star of the infernal regions (Satan) will rage more violently than ever and will cause frightful destruction, because he knows that his time is short, and because he sees that already many have gathered around my Sign. Over these he has no spiritual power, although he will kill the bodies of many; but through these sacrifices, **my power to lead the remnant host to victory will increase**...*

*The devil has power over all people **who do not trust** in my Heart...*

Third Vision: June 25, 1946

***I am the powerful Mediatrix of Grace**. It is the will of the Father that the world acknowledges this position of His Handmaid... God wants it so...*

In secret I shall work marvels in souls until the required number of victim souls will be filled. Upon you it depends to shorten the days of darkness. *Your blood and your sacrifices shall destroy the image of the beast. Then I can manifest myself to the world for the glory of the Almighty. Choose my Sign, so that the Triune God may soon be adored and honored.*

Pray and offer sacrifices through me. Pray always; pray the Rosary. Make all your entreaties to the Father through my Immaculate Heart... Keep the Saturdays, which have been dedicated to me, as I have requested.

... If you consecrate yourselves without reserve, I shall take care of all the rest. Crosses weighty and deep as the sea I shall lay upon my children, because I love them in my Sacrificed Son. I beseech you, be prepared to carry the cross that peace may soon be achieved.

I urge my people to fulfill my wishes quickly, because today more than ever such fulfillment of my will is necessary for God's greater honor and glory. The Father pronounces a dreadful woe upon all who refuse to obey His Will.

Our Lady of Akita

In 1973, Our Lady appeared to visionary and stigmatist, Sr. Agnes Sasagawa of Akita, Japan, in what has since been recognized as a Church-approved apparition, asking her to call upon the Eucharistic and Sacred Heart of Jesus and His Mother to help us pass through this time of upheaval and transition into the era of His New Kingdom. Mary said to say this prayer:

Most Sacred Heart of Jesus, truly present in the Holy Eucharist, I consecrate my body and soul to be entirely one with Your Heart being sacrificed at every instant on all the altars of the world and giving praise to the Father, pleading for the coming of His Kingdom. Please receive this humble offering of myself. Use me *as You will for the glory of the Father and the salvation of souls. Most Holy Mother of God, **never let me be separated from your Divine Son. Please defend and protect me** as your special child. Amen.*

On October 13, 1973, which is the anniversary of the 1917 miracle of Fatima, Our Lady of Akita gave a most serious prophecy about the difficult events that would soon occur, stating as follows:

*As I told you, if men do not repent and better themselves, the Father will inflict **a terrible punishment** on all humanity. It will be a punishment **greater than the deluge**, such as one will never have seen before. **Fire will fall from the sky** and will wipe out a great part of humanity, the good as well as the bad, sparing neither priests nor faithful. The survivors will find themselves so desolate that they will envy the dead. The only arms which will remain for you will be **the Rosary and the Sign** left by my Son. Each day, recite the prayers of the Rosary. With the Rosary, pray for the Pope, the bishops and the priests. The work of **<u>the devil will infiltrate even into the Church</u>** in such a way that one will see **cardinals opposing cardinals**, and bishops against other bishops. The priests who venerate me will be scorned and opposed by their Confreres. The churches and altars will be sacked. **The Church will be full of those who accept compromises** and the demon will press many priests and consecrated souls to leave the service of the Lord. The demon will rage especially against souls consecrated to God. The thought of the loss of so many souls is the cause of* *my sadness. If sins increase in number and gravity, there will no longer be pardon for them.*

The Virgin of Cuapa

Our Lady appeared to Church sacristan Bernardo Martinez in 1980 in Cuapa, Nicaragua. The Bishop positively affirmed the apparitions in 1982. Our Lady said:

> *Renew the **five first Saturdays**. You received many graces when all of you did this... If you don't change, you will hasten the coming of **the Third World War**.*

The Virgin Mary encouraged Bernardo Martinez to say this prayer:

> *St. Mary of Victory, Favorite Daughter of **God the Father**, give me your **faith**;*
>
> *Mother of **God the Son**, give me your **hope**;*
>
> *Sacred Spouse of **God the Holy Spirit**, give me your **charity** and cover us with your mantle.*

She requested that she be invoked with these words:

> *Holy Virgin, you are my Mother, the Mother to all of us sinners.*

The Flame of Love of the Immaculate Heart of Mary

Elizabeth Kindelmann was a *"victim soul"* seer who was born in Budapest. She and her husband had six children (1931 – 1942). In 1946, her husband died. In 1948, the Communist Nationalization of Hungary fired her for political reasons (having a statue of the Blessed Mother in her home). She started keeping a diary. Her diary begins on July 13, 1960. It speaks of three years of spiritual darkness (1958 –

1961) that prepared her for divine locutions (times when God would speak to her in private revelations). A decisive moment came on July 16, 1961, the feast of Our Lady of Mount Carmel (Elizabeth was a lay Carmelite) when the Heavenly communications given by Our Lord and Our Lady to Elizabeth Kindelmann began, and they continued between the years 1961 and 1982. Elizabeth's Spiritual Diary was written at the request of Our Lord Jesus. She died in 1985.

Recently, Cardinal Peter Erdo, Archbishop Primate of Budapest (and President of the Council of Episcopal Conferences in Europe), recognized her writings and gave her diary the Church's Imprimatur (June 6, 2009). The *"Flame of Love"* messages urge the world to **embrace Total Consecration to Jesus through Mary**. Elizabeth's writings show us that God chose Mary as His means to unite Himself with all humanity through His Son, Our Savior, Jesus Christ. More information on the Church-approved *"Flame of Love"* messages is available at www.TheFlameOfLove.org. Here are some pertinent excerpts from her *Flame of Love of the Immaculate Heart of Mary* messages:

The New Kingdom

From Jesus: *"All are invited to join my special fighting force.* ***The coming of my Kingdom must be your only purpose in life.*** *My words will reach a multitude of souls. Trust! I will help all of you in a miraculous way."*

He continues, *"Do not love comfort. Do not be cowards. Do not wait. Confront the storm to save souls. Give yourself to the work.* ***If*** *you do nothing, you abandon the earth to Satan and to sin.* *Open your eyes and see all the dangers that claim victims and threaten your own souls."*

Mary's Greatest Miracle

From Mary: *"**My Flame of Love is burning**. It is so great that I cannot keep it any longer within me. It leaps out of you with explosive power. When it pours out, **my love will destroy the satanic hatred that contaminates the world**. The greatest number of souls will be set free. Nothing like this has existed before. **This is my greatest miracle that I will do for all.** My words are crystal clear. Do not misinterpret them. Otherwise, you would be responsible. Act quickly, do not postpone my Cause for another day."* Satan looked on with his arms folded. He sensed that the Flame of Love is already lit. This produced his terrible fury.

Spread This Flame of Love – Heart to Heart

From Mary: *"**Take this flame** ... it's the flame of love of my Heart. **Ignite your own heart with it, and pass it on to others!** This flame full of blessings springing from my Immaculate Heart, and that I am giving you, must go from **heart to heart**. It will be **the great miracle** of light blinding Satan. It is the fire of love and concord. I obtained this grace on your behalf from the Eternal Father by virtue of the five Blessed Wounds of my Divine Son."*

Spread the Flame of Mary's Heart

From Mary: *"**Enter into battle. My Flame of Love will blind Satan to the degree that you spread it to the whole world.** This Flame will work miracles in their hearts. They will communicate this miracle to* *others. No need for this miracle to be authenticated. I will authenticate the miracle in each soul. All will recognize the outpouring of the Flame of Love."*

Mary's Flame of Love from Her Heart is <u>the NEW ARK!</u>

Elizabeth once asked: *"What is the Flame of Love?"* Jesus answered: *"The Flame of Love of my Mother is for you **what the Ark was for Noah!**"* And the Virgin Mary added: *"The Flame of Love of my Immaculate Heart **is Jesus Christ Himself!**"*

New Petition to the 'Hail Mary'

From Mary: *"When you pray the Hail Mary, include the following petition: '**Spread the effect of the grace of your Flame of Love over all of humanity.**'"* When the bishop asked why this should be done, Jesus explained, *"Because of the Holy Virgin's efficacious pleas, **the Most Blessed Trinity granted the outpouring of the Flame of Love**. For her sake, you must place this prayer in the Hail Mary."*

To the Lukewarm

From Jesus: *"To you who are lukewarm. How can I gain your attention? You no longer come to me in confidence. You are content with the passing things of earth, when I want you to come to me."* After this, Jesus said to me, *"Record my complaints. **Perhaps, when they read it, their hard hearts will be inflamed.** I wish I had to complain only about a few."*

Satan's Fire

From Jesus: *"If a fire begins, do not people put it out? Why do you not put out Satan's fire? How many look on in cowardice? They will be responsible. **They close their eyes and let souls be condemned.** Oh,* consecrated souls **do not be lazy**. *Laziness is the root of every evil in your soul. It leads to despair and you are unaware of its presence... Satan's implacable hatred is increasing to such an extent that **he even succeeds in gaining over pious souls**."*

Jesus then spoke of Elizabeth's martyrdom: *"Your inner martyrdom is My Will and Satan cannot stop it. This inner battle brings forth great fruit, just as external martyrdom does. **You must never be half-hearted**."*

Saving Families Depends on Us

From Mary: *"With my Flame of Love I want the home to come alive again with love. I want to unite scattered families. Help me! **My Flame of Love being lit depends on you**."*

Blinding Satan

From Mary: *"If people assist at Mass without any obligation and are in God's grace, **I will pour out the Flame of Love and blind Satan during Mass**. When Satan is blinded, he can do nothing. **Participating in Mass helps the most in blinding Satan**. He knows his downfall is near."*

Souls Going to Hell

From Mary: *"You (Elizabeth) are a mother. What if your six children were condemned to hell? What sorrow would you experience! **Likewise, what torments I experience** to see so many of my children fall into hell. **Help me!**"* Elizabeth: My heart cringed with sorrow.

The Storm Is Here, The Volcano Is Erupting

From Mary: *"Know that the earth is like nature before **a storm**... It can also be compared to **a volcano** when it suddenly awakens,* *smothers, kills, and blinds everyone with the infernal smoke sprouting up and its falling ashes, whose seism destroys everything around. The deadly ashes full of sulfur want to blemish human souls created in the image of God."*

The Fight Is Real

From Mary: *"**The elect souls will have to fight the Prince of Darkness.** It will be a frightening storm – no, not a storm, but a hurricane devastating everything! He even wants to destroy the faith and confidence of the elect. **I will always be beside you** in the storm that is now brewing. I am your mother. I can help you and I want to! **You will see everywhere the light of my Flame of Love** sprouting out like **a flash of lightning** illuminating Heaven and earth, and with which I will inflame even the dark and languid souls! But what sorrow it is for me to have to watch so many of my children throw themselves in hell!"*

A New World Is Coming

"Jolts" were coming to the Earth, Elizabeth said she was told by the Lord, jolts that will *"give rise to **a new world** by the power of faith."* The earth will be renewed, *"for **never has such a flow of grace ever been given** since the Word became Flesh."*

Help Our Lady to Save the World!

From Mary: *"My children, the Arm of my Divine Son is ready to strike. I can barely hold it back. Help me! **If you invoke my Flame of Love, we can save the world together.**"*

At Rue du Bac and Fatima, God requested that the world give special devotion to Mary's Immaculate Heart. Now, God is offering a special grace of protection to those willing to accept, embrace, and spread His Mother's Flame of Love and the power given to her Immaculate Heart, of which God gave to her as Mother under the Cross of her Son. She is indeed **the New Ark**!

PRAYER GIVEN BY JESUS TO ELIZABETH

From Jesus: *"Through this prayer, Satan will be blind, and souls will not be led into sin."* To Jesus and Mary, we pray:

May our feet journey together.

May our hands gather in unity.

May our hearts beat in unison.

May our souls be in harmony.

May our thoughts be as one.

May our ears listen to the silence together.

May our glances profoundly penetrate each other.

May our lips pray together to gain mercy from the Eternal Father.

NEW PETITION TO THE 'HAIL MARY'

Hail Mary, full of grace, the Lord is with thee.
Blessed are thou among women, and blessed is the fruit of thy womb, Jesus.
Holy Mary, Mother of God, pray for us sinners,
flood the whole of humanity with the graces of your Flame of Love,
now and at the hour of our death. Amen.

II. OUR LADY'S PROPHECIES ABOUT THE UNITED STATES

The Catholic Church in the United States names Mary as our

nation's patroness – under the title of the Immaculate Conception. Recall that Christopher Columbus had Our Lady's name on one of his ships. This country has been consecrated to Mary's Immaculate Conception from our foundations. The Mississippi River was originally called the *"River of the Immaculate Conception"*. The Basilica of the Immaculate Conception in Washington D.C. is one of the most beautiful shrines in the world. In 1792, Bishop John Carroll proclaimed Mary as the Patroness of America. Then in 1846, the Catholic Bishops of the United States assembled to officially proclaim *"Mary Immaculate"* as our nation's patroness:

> *We take this occasion, brethren, to communicate to you the determination, unanimously adopted by us, to place ourselves and all entrusted to our charge throughout the United States, **under the special patronage of the holy Mother of God**, whose **Immaculate Conception** is venerated by the piety of the faithful throughout the Catholic Church. By the aid of her prayers, we entertain the **confident hope** that we will be strengthened to perform the arduous duties of our ministry, and that you will be enabled to practice the sublime virtues, of which her life presents the most perfect example.*

This was eight years before the dogmatic proclamation from Rome declaring Mary the Immaculate Conception. The United States not only has a strong Catholic history, but also a strong Marian history that we need to bring back to light with new fervor in these times. There are several approved apparitions regarding our country, including some as follows.

Our Lady of Good Help

The Virgin Mary appeared in the United States in 1859, just one year after she appeared in France to St. Bernadette Soubirous as Our Lady of Lourdes. At Champion, Wisconsin, Our Lady identified herself to an American immigrant girl named Adele Brice as the *"Queen of Heaven"* in what would become the Church-approved apparition of Our Lady of Good Help. The Message of Our Lady to Adele was simple, just an instruction and a promise. But, the underlying prophetic aspect of this apparition, and specifically regarding related events that took place in the area soon afterwards, applies well to us in these times. Our Lady said:

> *I am the Queen of Heaven, who prays for the conversion of sinners, and I wish you to do the same. You received Holy Communion this morning, and that is well. But **you must do more**. Make a general confession, and offer Communion for the conversion of sinners. If they do not convert and do penance, my Son will be obliged to punish them.*

Turning to the women with Adele, Our Lady said:

> *Blessed are they that believe without seeing. **What are you doing here in idleness**…while your companions are working in the vineyard of my Son?*

Our Lady continued to Adele saying:

> *Gather the children in this wild country and teach them what they should know for salvation. Teach them their catechism, how to sign themselves with the sign of the Cross, and how to approach the sacraments; that is what I wish you to do. Go and*

fear nothing. I will help you.

Exactly twelve years later, after the initial apparition, Our Lady demonstrated her presence with a miracle. By this time, Adele had become a religious sister. In 1871, a raging wildfire swept through Wisconsin destroying many of the settlements in the area. It was one of the worst in U.S. history. Rather than flee for their lives, Sister Adele and the faithful rushed to the shrine of Our Lady of Good Help. **They went to Mary for help!** The fire completely surrounded the shrine, but rather than panic in fear, they turned toward Our Lady and prayed. **The fire engulfed everything** in all directions, even singeing the fence around the shrine on all sides, **but the shrine, and the small plot of land it stood on were left untouched**. In this miracle, Our Lady seems to be telling us today that we can be protected from the spiritual, economic, social, and possibly actual firestorms that will soon engulf our times. And she says we must return to teaching the truths of the Faith; and do even more, offering sacrifices for sinners.

Our Lady of America

In the United States, Our Lady has given messages for our times and for our country to Sister Mary Ephrem (Mildred Neuzil), who died on January 10, 2000. This devotion to the Blessed Virgin Mary under the title of Our Lady of America enjoys canonical approval through former Archbishop of Cincinnati, Ohio, the late Paul Francis Leibold. Furthermore, many other Bishops have also shown their approval by their promotion of this devotion. The Most Reverend Raymond L. Burke, (former) Archbishop of Saint Louis, a premier canon lawyer of the Church, issued a public opinion on Our Lady of America. In his letter dated May 31, 2007, he reviewed the history of Our Lady of America and the actions of Archbishop Leibold approving this devotion.

Sr. Mary Ephram was told by Our Lady of America: *"America, the United States in particular, is being given the tremendous, yet privileged opportunity to lead all nations in a spiritual renewal never before so necessary, so important, so vital."* Mary said that she was coming to America now as a last resort. Sr. Mary Ephram said that Mary *"promised that **greater miracles than those granted at Lourdes and Fatima** would be granted here in America, the United States in particular, if we would do as she desires."* Mary promised great *"miracles of the soul."* Our Lady taught Sr. Mary Ephram to pray:

"By your Holy and Immaculate Conception,
O Mary, deliver us from evil."

On the fifty-third anniversary of Our Lady of America, Our Lady told Sr. Mary Ephram: *"From the beginning of time every prophecy, every vision, throughout the centuries, will have its fulfillment in Our Lady of America and her message of **the Indwelling Trinity living in every soul**, which **will renew the whole world and destroy Lucifer** and all the evil spirits in the fight he is making against the Indwelling Trinity."*

About purity, Our Lady says: *"I am Our Lady of America. I desire that my children honor me, especially by **the purity of their lives.**"* She said: *"Dear child, **evil is so insidious that it often passes for good**. The simple and pure of heart alone can detect the* *difference... Many **unnatural acts** are being committed in the name of love. This evil is being **disguised and tolerated as an intrinsic right** like any other. Even some of **My priests and consecrated virgins** are being caught up in this web of evil – not realizing the terrible consequences... Many **false doctrines** are being taught and for many the true Christ is never made known. The **false prophets** and self-proclaimed messiahs are drawing many away from Me."*

She speaks of the pivotal role of the United States – for good or for evil – in our times, saying:

*It is the United States that is to lead the world to **peace**, the peace of Christ, the peace that He brought with Him from heaven... Dear children, unless the United States accepts and carries out faithfully the mandate given to it by heaven to lead the world to peace, there will come upon it and all nations **a great havoc of war and incredible suffering**. If, however, the United States is faithful to this mandate from heaven and yet fails in the pursuit of peace because the rest of the world will not accept or cooperate, then the United States will not be burdened with the punishment about to fall.*

Weep, then, dear children, weep with your mother over the sins of men... Intercede with me before the throne of mercy, for sin is overwhelming the world and punishment is not far away.

*It is **the darkest hour**, but if men will come to me, my Immaculate Heart will make it bright again with the mercy which my Son will rain down through my hands. Help me save those who will not save themselves. Help me bring once again* *the sunshine of God's peace upon the world.*

*If my desires are not fulfilled much suffering will come to this land. My faithful one, if my warnings are taken seriously and enough of my children strive constantly and faithfully to renew and reform themselves in their inward and outward lives, then there will be no **nuclear war**. What happens to the world depends upon those who live in it. There must be much more good than evil prevailing in order to prevent the holocaust that is so near approaching. Yet I tell you, my daughter, even should such a destruction happen because there were not enough souls who took my warning seriously, there will remain **a remnant**, untouched by the chaos who, having been **faithful in following me and spreading my warnings**, will gradually inhabit the earth again with their dedicated and holy lives.*

Our Lady of America is calling the United States to lead the world, to establish peace, to restore the virtue of purity, and to protect the family.

A special request from Heaven: Our Lady of America is requesting the U.S. Bishops to process in solemn procession with her statue into the National Basilica of the Immaculate Conception in Washington D.C. and crown her. Our Lady said that **if this is done**, the United States of America would turn back toward morality and the national shrine would become a place of *"wonders."* It is very late now, but it is not too late. Let us turn to Our Lady of America and ask for her to be enshrined in the National Basilica of the United States, that this prophecy might be fulfilled for good.

Our Lady of America is calling the United States to lead the world, to establish peace, to restore the virtue of purity, and to protect the family. She calls for us to renew the family by inviting **the Most Holy Trinity to be the center of the Christian family**, and **to recognize the Holy Family of Joseph, Mary, and Jesus as the model of family life**. Let us honor Our Lady of America as she requests, so that she might bring faith and hope to our world and to families!

Our Lady of All Nations about America

In the apparitions to Ida Peerdeman, Our Lady of All Nations spoke a prophecy about America, saying: *"I will set my foot down in the midst of the world and show you: that is America"*, and then, [Our Lady] immediately pointed to another part, saying, *"Manchuria—there will be tremendous insurrections."* Ida then wrote: *"I see Chinese marching, and a line which they are crossing."* This seems to be some kind of prophecy about the U.S. being harmed by China.

Other Prophecies about Coming War and Persecution

Sr. Elena Aiello was declared *"Blessed"* on September 14, 2011, the Feast of the Exultation of the Holy Cross, by Pope Benedict XVI, just about a year before his retirement. Blessed Elena was a Mystic, Victim Soul, Prophetess, and Foundress of the Minim Tertiaries of the Passion of Our Lord Jesus Christ. From 1940 to 1961, Jesus and Mary gave many messages to Bl. Elena in Italy. She was a stigmatist who bore the wounds of Christ in her hands, feet and side.

In 1940, Sister Elena was directed by the Lord to deliver a message to Premier Benito Mussolini, telling him not to join with Hitler in World War II. Otherwise, Italy would suffer a terrible defeat and Mussolini would be punished by Divine Justice and have a speedy downfall. But he ignored the warning, and all that was foretold came to pass. Bl. Elena's prophecies appear to be directly related to Fatima and many other modern Marian prophecies. Some of her prophecies include:

April 7, 1950 Good Friday:

Satan reigns and triumphs on earth!

"See how **Russia will burn!**" Before my eyes there extended an immense field covered with flames and smoke, in which souls were submerged as if in a sea of fire! "And all this **fire**," concluded the Madonna, "Is not that which will fall from the hands of men, but will be hurled directly from the Angels. Therefore, **I ask prayers, penance and sacrifice**, so I may act as Mediatrix for My Son in order to save souls."

April 16, 1954 Good Friday:

The Madonna appeared to me. She was dressed in black, with seven swords piercing Her Immaculate Heart. Coming closer, with an expression of profound sorrow, and with tears on her cheeks, she spoke to me, saying: '**Listen attentively, and reveal to all**:

...Soon the world will be afflicted with great calamities, bloody revolutions, frightful hurricanes, and the overflowing of streams and the seas... if men do not return to God with prayers and penances, the world will be overturned in **a new and more terrible war**. Arms most deadly will destroy peoples and nations! The *dictators of the earth, specimens infernal, **will demolish the churches and desecrate the Holy Eucharist**, and will destroy things most dear. In this impious war, much will be destroyed of that which has been built by the hands of man.*

CLOUDS WITH LIGHTNING, FLASHES OF FIRE IN THE SKY, AND A TEMPEST OF FIRE SHALL FALL UPON THE WORLD. THIS TERRIBLE SCOURGE, NEVER BEFORE SEEN IN THE HISTORY OF HUMANITY, WILL LAST SEVENTY HOURS. GODLESS PERSONS WILL BE CRUSHED AND WIPED OUT. MANY WILL BE LOST BECAUSE THEY REMAIN IN THEIR OBSTINACY OF SIN. THEN SHALL BE SEEN THE POWER OF LIGHT OVER THE POWER OF DARKNESS.

*Prayers and penances are necessary because men MUST RETURN TO GOD and **to My Immaculate Heart**—the Mediatrix of men to God, and thus the world will be at least in part saved.*

April 8, 1955 Good Friday:

*LAUNCH FORTH INTO THE WORLD **A MESSAGE** TO MAKE KNOWN TO ALL THAT THE SCOURGE IS NEAR AT HAND.*

The justice of God is weighing upon the world. Mankind, defiled in the mire, soon will be washed in its own blood, by disease; by famine; by earthquakes; by cloudbursts, tornadoes, floods, and terrible storms; and by war.

...If men do not amend their ways, a terrifying scourge of fire will come down from Heaven upon all the nations of the world, and men will be punished according to the debts contracted with Divine justice. There will be frightful moments for all, because

Heaven will be joined with the earth, and all the un-Godly people will be destroyed, SOME NATIONS WILL BE PURIFIED, WHILE OTHERS WILL DISAPPEAR ENTIRELY.

*You are to **transmit these warnings to all**, in order that the new generation will know that men had been warned in time to turn to God by doing penance, and thus **could have avoided these punishments**.*

December 8, 1956 Feast of the Immaculate Conception:

The times are grievous. The whole world is in turmoil, because it has become worse than AT THE TIME OF THE DELUGE!"

***Launch at once a message into the world**, to advise men **to return to God** by prayers and penances, and to come with confidence **to my Immaculate Heart**. My intercession must be shown, because I am the Mother of God, of the just, and of sinners. Through prayer and penance, my mercy will be able to hold back the hand of God's justice.*

1959:

***Russia will march upon all the nations of Europe, particularly Italy, and will raise her flag over the Dome of St. Peter's.** Italy will be severely tried by a great revolution, and Rome will be purified in blood for its many sins, especially those of impurity! The flock is about to be dispersed and the Pope must suffer greatly!*

August 22, 1960 Feast of the Immaculate Heart:

If the people do not recognize in these scourges the warnings of Divine Mercy, and do not return to God with truly Christian living,

ANOTHER TERRIBLE WAR WILL COME FROM THE EAST TO THE WEST. ***RUSSIA WITH HER SECRET ARMIES WILL BATTLE AMERICA; WILL OVERRUN EUROPE.***

1961 Good Friday:

Oh, what a horrible vision I see! A great revolution is going on in Rome! They are entering **the Vatican**. *The Pope is all alone; he is praying. They are holding the Pope. They take him by force. They knock him down to the floor. They are trying him. Oh God! Oh, God! They are kicking him. What a horrible scene! How dreadful! Our Blessed Mother is drawing near. Like corpses those evil men fall down to the floor. Our Lady helps the Pope to his feet and, taking him by the arm, she covers him with her mantle saying: 'Fear not!' My daughter, Rome will not be saved, because the Italian rulers have forsaken the Divine Light and because only a few people really love the Church. But the day is not far off when all the wicked shall perish, under the tremendous blows of Divine Justice…* **The powers of evil** *are getting ready to strike furiously in every part of the globe. Tragic events are in store for the future. For quite a while, and in many a way, I have warned the world… If possible,* **publish this message throughout the world, and admonish all the people to do penance and to return right away to God.**

Jesus and Mary are in so many ways trying to warn and prepare us for the times that are now at hand. May we respond now!

CHAPTER 4

Jesus Invites Us to Enter the New Ark
of Safety and Victory –
The Immaculate Heart of Mary

*Then another sign appeared in the sky; it was **a huge red dragon**…*
*Then the dragon stood **before the Woman** about to give birth,*
*to **devour her child** when she gave birth.*
Revelation 12:3-4

It was through the Blessed Virgin Mary that Jesus came into the
*world, and it is also **through her that He must reign** in the world.*
St. Louis de Montfort

***God wishes to establish** throughout the world*
devotion to my Immaculate Heart…
*in the end **my Immaculate Heart will triumph.***
Our Lady of Fatima

In the time of the Flood of Noah, all who entered the ark were
saved by God. Today, God has provided a new ark, and all who enter it
will be saved. Noah's ark is a symbol of the Church, but also of Mary.
Noah's ark was the means to transition from the old to the new
covenant and renewed world. So too is Mary's Heart in these times.
The New Ark of safety and protection is Our Lady's Immaculate

Heart. Let us pray to recognize this Gift and then to enter willingly and quickly. Let us gather together and bring others into the New Ark.

The last great spiritual battle has begun, and the lines have been drawn between the dragon and the Woman. She is calling her children to fight. God is sending the most important human person in Heaven to give us **the most important Message in the history of the Church**, since the time of Christ, concerning **the fulfillment of the final biblical prophecies**. Mary is coming from Heaven to explain the Signs of the Times. God is sending Mary **to open the Book of the Apocalypse,** and to reveal its mysteries **in our times, because *we* are the generation of its fulfillment.**

The final battle has indeed begun. Like never before in history, man is on the verge of inflicting genocide on humanity to such a scale that the world's population will be depleted in huge proportions. We must ask God to intervene, and He will. What is needed now is a divine intervention. All the prophecies in the Book of Revelation will now unfold in the world.

In these times, God is asking His people to enter the **Immaculate Heart of His Mother,** because **she is the Ark of the New Covenant.** At the time of Noah, immediately before the flood, those whom the Lord had destined to survive His terrible chastisement entered into the ark. In these our times, God is sending Our Lady to invite all her children to enter into the Ark of the New Covenant which she has built **in her Immaculate Heart. There is happening today what happened in the days of the flood,** and no one is giving a thought to what is awaiting them. As Jesus warned: *"For as it was in the days of*

Noah, so it will be at the coming of the Son of Man." Everyone is much occupied in thinking only of themselves, of their own earthly interests, of pleasures and of satisfying in every sort of way, their own disordinate passions. But, the warning has been given; we must quickly enter the New Ark while the door is still open!

The Heavenly Father's Secret Gift for Our Times

Mary's Immaculate Heart – This is the heavenly Father's **secret Gift as part of His Plan for the salvation of the world**. Sr. Lucia of Fatima was given profound insights concerning the Immaculate Heart and God's Plan for our times. She wrote:

> *God is giving **two last remedies to the world**. These are **the Holy Rosary and the Devotion to the Immaculate Heart of Mary**... the **two means to save the world are prayer and** sacrifice... Finally, **devotion to the Immaculate Heart of Mary**, Our Most holy Mother, consists in considering Her as the seat of mercy, of goodness and of pardon and as the certain door by which we are to enter Heaven.*

Just before she died, little Bl. Jacinta of Fatima, whose body is now incorrupt, pleaded with Lucia, saying:

> *Lucia, **tell everybody that God gives graces through the Immaculate Heart of Mary**. Tell them to ask graces from her, and that the Heart of Jesus wishes to be venerated together with the Immaculate Heart of Mary. Ask them to plead for peace from the Immaculate Heart of Mary, for **the Lord has confided the peace of the world to her**.*

John Paul II explains:

> ***Devotion to Mary's Immaculate Heart*** *expresses our reverence for her maternal compassion, both for Jesus and for all of us, her spiritual children, as she stood at the foot of the Cross... devotion to Mary's heart* **has prime importance,** *for through love of her Son and of all of humanity she exercises a unique instrumentality in bringing us to him.*

Recall that Our Lady of America said:

> **It is the darkest hour,** *but if men will come to me,* **my Immaculate Heart** *will make it bright again with the mercy which my Son will rain down through my hands.* **Help me save those who will not save themselves.** *Help me bring once again the sunshine of God's peace upon the world.*

Mary – The New Ark, the Safe Haven of These <u>Apocalyptic</u> Times

God is sending Mary to be the New Ark of protection and safety:

- *And the temple of God was opened in heaven, and there was seen in his temple* ***the ark*** *of his testament: and there were lightnings, and voices, and thunderings, and an earthquake, and great hail. A* ***great sign*** *appeared in the sky,* ***a woman*** *(Mary) clothed with the* ***sun,*** *with the* ***moon*** *under her feet, and on her head a crown of twelve* ***stars.*** *(Revelation 11-12)*

- Our Lady offers to all humanity the safe haven in the middle of this war – her Immaculate Heart.

Was Noah (or his family) harmed in the Flood? Did he have any problems? Were all his needs taken care of? So too for those who today consecrate themselves and their families to the Immaculate Heart of Mary in these times. Do you understand the Message God is trying to tell you? All those in the ark during the time of the Flood of Noah survived! Eight people survived that Flood. And all those who are in the New Ark will 'survive' this new Flood of our times. When the atomic bomb was dropped on Hiroshima at the end of WWII, eight priests who were living at the epicenter of the blast miraculously survived. They had only one explanation: ***"We believe that we survived because we were living the Message of Fatima… In our house, the Holy Rosary was recited together everyday."*** In other words, they had entered and were spiritually living in the New Ark, and thus, they were protected and saved, from even an atomic blast. So too it will be for us today, in this modern time of a new Hiroshima. Put your hope in that! Mary Reconciler of the People and Nations, in approved apparitions to Servant of God **Maria Esperanza** of Betania (1980s), says: *"Fill yourselves with* **gratitude***… since the Holy Spirit will enlighten each one of you* **_in these apocalyptic times_***… in the light of* **the New Dawn** *of my Divine Jesus. He, my Beloved Son, wishes for all of you to* **live cradled in [my] motherly Heart***, with the charisma and graces of the Holy Spirit…* **My Heart I give to you!***"*

Ven. Magdalene Porzat

Magdalene Porzat was a humble, illiterate, and aged country maid in France in the 19th century. She received Church-regarded prophecy about the times at hand and God's call to enter the New Ark of Mary's Heart. She states as follows:

> *Listen my children, to what Mary our Mother charges me to announce to you. **'Behold the end of time!'**... Behold now the Father and the Son, to console us, send us **the Triumphant Spirit with Mary as His Spouse**. This is a grand miracle... Mary comes from heaven. She comes accompanied by a legion of angels. I announce to you **the seven crises**, the seven wounds and sorrows of Mary, which should have to precede her triumph and our cure, namely:*
>
> *1. Inclemencies of seasons and inundations*
> *2. Diseases to animals and plants*
> *3. Cholera over men*
> *4. Revolutions*
> *5. Wars*
> *6. A universal bankruptcy*
> *7. Confusion*
>
> *...Men shall believe all is lost and annihilated... Whoever is not on the bark of Peter shall be engulfed. [Then] **the ark (of Mary's Heart) comes out of the storm and a calm ensues**... Behold there is confusion; confusion even in the sanctuary... Well! Mary comes to harvest the elect from the earth... A grand event shall have to take place in order to terrify the wicked... **After this... All shall be good.** The Pharisees will be the last to be converted... The Jews who have refused to receive Jesus Christ in his humiliation will acknowledge Him at the glorious arrival of Mary..."*
>
> *The dove (Mary, with the Spirit) comes to us from Heaven, wearing on her breast a white cross, sign of reconciliation and*

waving a sword of fire, symbol of love. <u>*She seats herself on a*</u> <u>*throne of solid gold,*</u> **<u>figure of Noah's ark</u>***; for she comes to announce* **the end of a deluge of evils**. *Behold,* **she comes, our Mother!**... *Behold the Immaculate conception of* **the Kingdom of God** *that precedes the arrival of Jesus Christ. It is the mansion of God upon earth, which is going to purify and prepare itself to receive the Emmanuel. Jesus Christ cannot come into this hovel of the world... It is necessary that God should send His Spirit to renew the face of the earth by means of* **another creation**, *to render it a worthy mansion for the God made man.*

Behold here the fire from below, for burning and changing everything. Behold here the fire from above! **The love of God comes to embrace and transfigure the world.** *I see the earth rendered level, its valleys are raised; its mountains are lowered; there is nothing more than gentle hills and beautiful vales. Since I am as I am, I see nothing else before us, but* **union and universal fraternity. All men are in reciprocal love. One helps the other. They are all happy.**

Enter NOW into the Ark of Mary's Heart

It is time we gather together in the spiritual **cenacle of Mary's Immaculate Heart**. Let us pray that the Holy Spirit will bring us to the understanding of the whole and entire truth; that He will bring us into **the secret** of the word of God and will give us the light of wisdom to understand all the Gospel and whatever is described in it concerning the times through which we are living. The Holy Spirit will help us understand **the signs of our time** – the times foretold by Holy Scripture as those of **the great apostasy, the false prophet and of the coming of the Antichrist**. These are times of **great tribulation** and of innumerable sufferings for all, which will bring us to live through these final events in preparation for the **Second Coming** of Jesus in glory and the new Era of Peace on earth.

We must not be troubled. The times of the purification, of the great tribulation, of the apostasy, and of the chastisement have arrived. This is why God is sending Our Lady to call us all today to **enter into the tabernacle of her Immaculate Heart**, so that she may offer us as a perfect gift to the glory of the Most Holy Trinity. Mary's **Immaculate Heart** will become your strongest defense, the shield of protection that will safeguard you from every attack of the Adversary.

The Sorrowful and Immaculate Heart of Mary –
"Mother of the Sorrowful Heart"

Around the same time as Fatima, Our Lord appeared to Franciscan Tertiary, Belgian mystic, stigmatist, and the Apostle of the Devotion to the Sorrowful and Immaculate Heart of Mary, Berthe Petit. Cardinal Mercier of Belgium and Cardinal Bourne of England recognized her writings and were among her devotees. Based on Cardinal Mercier's advice to mention the devotion promoted by Berthe, Pope Benedict XV, in May 1915, ended a letter to the bishops of the world with a recommendation to seek the intercession of the *"Sorrowful and Immaculate Heart of Mary"*. Berthe received a vision of the Hearts of

Jesus and Mary closely united together, pierced by a sword, which was accompanied by words from Jesus:

> *Teach souls to love the Heart of my Mother pierced with the sorrow that transfixed My own Heart.*

Berthe was also taught that we should strive to *"live in the Heart of Mary"* as she lived in that of Christ, and to make known the love of Mary's Heart. She saw the Hearts of Jesus and Mary interpenetrating each other, and hovering over the Two Hearts was a Dove (Holy Spirit). Jesus then said:

> *You must think of My Mother's Heart as you think of Mine; **live in this Heart** as you seek to live in Mine; give yourself to this Heart as you give yourself to Mine. You must **spread the love of this Heart** so wholly united to Mine.*

And Our Lady reveals the dearest title she has been given by her Son, saying: *"Understand the sorrows which my Heart endured and the sufferings of my whole being for the salvation of the world... I call myself, **'Mother of the Sorrowful Heart'**. This title willed by my Son, is **dear to me above all other of my titles**. According as it is spread everywhere, there will be granted graces of mercy, spiritual renewal, and salvation."*

Jesus said to Berthe:

> ***The time has now arrived when I wish mankind to turn to the Sorrowful and Immaculate Heart of My Mother.*** *Let this prayer be uttered by every soul: **'Sorrowful and Immaculate Heart of Mary, pray for us'** so that it may spread as a refreshing and purifying balm of reparation that will appease My anger. **This***

devotion to the Sorrowful and Immaculate Heart of My Mother *will restore faith and hope to broken hearts and to ruined families. It will help to repair the destruction. It will sweeten sorrow. It will be **a new strength** for My Church, bringing souls, not only to confidence in My Heart, but also to abandonment to the Sorrowful Heart of My Mother.*

Jesus continued, discussing that His own Triumph and New Reign would come through this devotion, saying:

It is through the Sorrowful and Immaculate Heart of My Mother that I will triumph, because having cooperated in the redemption of souls, this Heart has the right to share a similar cooperation in the manifestations of My justice and of My love. My Mother is noble in everything but she is especially so in her wounded Heart, transfixed by the wound of Mine.

Ven. Conchita

Our Lord taught Ven. Conchita (Concepion Cabrera de Armida), through her Church-recognized writings, the critical role He has given to His Mother for these times. Conchita writes Jesus' words about the New Era of the Spirit and the heart of Mary as follows:

*For these last times set aside for **the reign of the Holy Spirit**, it is reserved to honor the suffering of the solitude of **Mary, His Most Beloved Spouse**... Mary lived in order to be an instrument of the Holy Spirit in the fledgling Church. She [is] **Consoler, Protector, and Refuge of Sinners**... At the foot of the cross, her children were born. My death gave them **life in the heart of Mary**, but she,* *before dying, had to manifest that maternity on earth, purchasing infinite present and future graces for her children with the cruel sorrow of My absence... But now the time has come that these children will be her children and for their happiness, will **honor that broken heart**, with its sharpest, most significant sacrifices. Thus, **Mary purchased millions of graces** for each and every one of them and **it is time for them to be grateful to her**.*

*...**Now that the reign of the Holy Spirit is going to be renewed, as in a new Pentecost, Mary will shine** again... Mary will shine with a new sparkle before guilty humanity, winning over many hearts... Many saints have [begun to announce] a new surge of love for Mary and a greater knowledge of her virtues during these end times.*

Our Lord further instructed Ven. Conchita on the fact that the closer we draw to Mary, the more she helps us to imitate Christ. Jesus said: *"In my life for souls, My daughter, My Mother is never separated from Me; that is, the imitation of our lives on earth has to be simultaneous, although hers was founded on Mine. Moreover, just as I was the Redeemer, **she was the Co-Redeemer;** and the souls that love her more, and that make themselves more like her, are those that most perfectly take on My likeness."*

St. Maximilian Kolbe

St. Maximilian Maria Kolbe was also graced with a keen understanding of how vital Mary's role is in the lives of souls and how truly vital our relationship with her is, especially in these times. He wrote of Mary:

> We know so little as yet about all that the Immaculata has done for the human race, from the first instant of her existence to this very day... **Every grace given to us has passed through her hands**... And all this must be proposed to souls so that they may be **nourished with the Immaculata**... so that they might resemble her as soon as possible and be **changed into her**. Then they will <u>**love Jesus with the Immaculata's heart.**</u>

St. Kolbe was also given an understanding of the Immaculate Conception of Mary, as the spouse of the Holy Spirit, which helps confirm Ven. Conchita's summary. He stated:

> Among creatures made in God's image, the union brought about by married love is the most intimate of all. In a much more precise, more interior manner, **the Holy Spirit lives in the soul of the Immaculata**, in the depths of her very being. He makes her fruitful from the very first instant of her existence, all during her life, and for all eternity. This **eternal "Immaculate Conception"** (which is the Holy Spirit) produces, in an immaculate manner, divine life itself in the womb (or depths) of Mary's soul, making her the Immaculate Conception, the **human Immaculate Conception**. The virginal womb of Mary's body is kept sacred for him; there he conceives in time—because everything that is material happens in time—the human life of the man-God.

St. Louis de Montfort and the Age of Mary

St. Louis-Marie de Montfort, who has been proposed as a Doctor of the Church, prophesied about our times, saying:

> *Towards the end of the world... Almighty God and His Holy Mother are to raise up **great saints who will surpass in holiness most other saints** as the cedars of Lebanon tower over the little shrubs.*

How will the Lord do this? St. Louis de Montfort states, *"The Holy Spirit finding his dear spouse present again in souls, will come down into them with great power... that **age of Mary**, when many souls, **chosen by Mary** and given her by the most high God, will hide themselves completely in the depth of her soul, **becoming living copies of her**, loving and glorifying Jesus."*

How will this come about? It will come about when the world embraces the Will of God, as Jesus did and declared: *"I seek not my own will, but **the will of Him** who sent Me."* It will come about when we imitate Mary who declared to God: *"Behold I am the handmaid of the Lord, be it done unto me according to **Thy Will**."* It will come about when the world embraces living with the Gift of God's Will, living in the Divine Will, the Grace of all graces.

St. Louis de Montfort also was given this understanding of how God would use His Mother and the Holy Spirit to allow souls to live with this singular grace of graces. St. Louis de Montfort wrote:

> *Mary has produced together with the Holy Spirit, the greatest thing, which has been or ever will be, a God-man; and **she will consequently produce the greatest saints that there will be in the end of time.** The formation and education of the great saints who*

shall come at the end of the world are reserved for her. For it is only that singular and miraculous Virgin who can produce, in union with the Holy Spirit, singular and extraordinary things. They shall be great and exalted before God in **sanctity,** *superior to all other creatures by their* **lively zeal,** *and so well* **sustained with God's assistance that, with the humility of their heel, in union with Mary, they shall crush the head of the devil and cause Jesus Christ to triumph.**

What a great prophecy! It is about us! May his words come true concerning us in these times, for the glory of God. More information on St. Louis de Montfort's Total Consecration to Mary is available at www.MyConsecration.org.

Experience the Triumph & Reign of the Two Hearts

"I will commission my two witnesses to prophesy." (Revelation 11:3)

The world is about to enter **the New Era** of Peace and the Spirit, but only through the great tribulation and divine chastisement of purification. This will be the New Era of the Two Hearts, of the Triumph of the Immaculate Heart and the Reign of the Sacred Heart.

Go to the Two Hearts! As **the Angel of Fatima** said: ***"The Hearts of Jesus and Mary are attentive to the voice of your supplication."***

St. John Eudes, who St. Pius X calls the father, doctor, and apostle of the Hearts of Jesus and Mary Devotion, enunciates this doctrine saying: *"I shall only tell you that you must never separate what God has so perfectly united. So closely are Jesus and Mary bound up with each other that whoever beholds Jesus sees Mary; whoever loves*

Jesus, loves Mary; whoever has devotion to Jesus, has devotion to Mary." He continues elsewhere, saying:

> *Although the Heart of Jesus is distinct from that of Mary... and infinitely surpasses it in excellence and holiness nevertheless,* **God has so closely united these two Hearts that we may say with truth that They are but one**, *because They have always been animated with the same spirit and filled with the same sentiments and affections... Jesus is enshrined in the Heart of Mary so completely that in honoring and glorifying her Heart, we honor and glorify Jesus Christ Himself.*

As we mentioned earlier, the *"Miraculous Medal"* apparitions to St. Catherine really begin the Marian Age and the heavenly revelations of the Two Hearts. On the back of the medal, there was to be an *"M"* and a cross, with the Two Hearts of Jesus and Mary, all encircled by twelve stars, which is the Church – **the Church surrounding the Two Hearts**. Mary promised: *"All who wear it will receive great graces."*

Jesus also reportedly spoke to **Bl. Dina Belanger,** a Canadian Nun of the Congregation of Jesus and Mary who was born in 1897 and died in 1929 at the age of 33. He told her of His desire to reign in souls through the Immaculate Heart of Mary, so that the Two Hearts could reign and triumph together, saying:

> *No invocation (prayer) responds better to the immense desire of my Eucharistic Heart to **reign in souls** than:*
>
> **'Eucharistic Heart of Jesus, may Your kingdom come through the Immaculate Heart of Mary';**

and to my no less infinite desire to communicate my graces to souls than: 'Eucharistic Heart of Jesus, burning with love for us, inflame our hearts with love for You.'

The great gift of our times is the consecration to the Two Hearts. While the consecration is a most powerful devotion in itself, it must be lived with a spirit of self-reform and renunciation to bear fruit that will last.

The greatest secret that Heaven is revealing to us in these times is the secret of the Two Hearts. Heaven is telling us that the promise of safety and protection comes through devotion to the Two Hearts, especially when placed side by side.

The Two Hearts – Side by Side

Our Lady instructs us to enter into the safety and protection of her Immaculate Heart. Just as the Miraculous Medal apparition revealed, at Fatima, Our Lord Himself asks for the Two Hearts to be placed side by side. Shortly before her death, **Blessed Jacinta of Fatima** told her cousin Lucia:

*In a short time now I am going to heaven. You are to stay here and say that God wishes to establish in the world the devotion to the Immaculate Heart of Mary... Tell everybody that **God grants graces through the Immaculate Heart of Mary**, and that they must ask them from her. Tell them that **the Heart of Jesus wishes that by His side should be venerated the Immaculate Heart of Mary**. Tell them to ask peace through the Immaculate Heart of Mary; God has placed it in her hands. Oh that I could put into the* *heart of everybody the flame that I feel burning within my breast and which makes me love so much the Heart of Jesus and the Heart of Mary.*

And as Our Lord told Lucia of Fatima:

"Put the devotion of the Immaculate Heart besides the devotion of My Sacred Heart."

John Paul II also stated: *"In the History of Salvation therefore **the Two Hearts** are inseparably united, and this definitive alliance is integral to the Church's doctrine… to her piety and the liturgical celebration… and to her pastoral pedagogy."*

Bl. Mother Teresa of Calcutta explains the relation between the Two Hearts, saying: *"The Heart of Mary is the door which leads us directly to Jesus. **She is the gate through which we enter His Sacred Heart.** Each 'Hail Mary' we pray opens our heart to His love and leads us into a deeper union with the Eucharistic Heart of Jesus.*

The Era of Peace will usher in the Triumph of the Immaculate Heart of Mary and New Reign of the Sacred Heart of Jesus. Christ's new reign will *not* be one of a visible ruling over this world, but a spiritual ushering in the new Kingdom of the Divine Will. He will then reign in souls and be glorified by the whole created universe. This **New Era will coincide with the greatest Triumph of the Eucharistic Jesus** and with **the complete fulfillment of the Divine Will**. Thus, reader, let us look forward with HOPE to and prepare for **the Triumph and Reign of the Two Hearts, the great Era of Peace, and the establishing of the universal Kingdom of the Divine Will on earth**; and let us spread this 'good news' with urgency and love!

CHAPTER 5

Jesus Introduces The Grace of All Graces –
The Glory of Living in His Divine Will

*Yet I live, no longer I, but **Christ lives in me**;*
insofar as I now live in the flesh,
I live by faith in the Son of God
who has loved me and given Himself up for me.
St. Paul in Galatians 2:20

*Christ enables us **to live in Him** all that He Himself lived,*
*and **He lives it in us**.*
Catechism of the Catholic Church

At the Second Vatican Council, the Bishops offered the following understanding of how God unfolds His plan and how we are to accept and experience God's plan in our lives:

*By faith **man freely commits his entire self to God**, making "the full submission of his intellect and will to God who reveals," and willingly assenting to the Revelation given by him. Before this faith can be exercised, man must have **the*** *grace of God to move and assist him; he must have **the interior helps of the Holy Spirit**, who moves the heart and converts it to God, who opens the eyes of the mind and "makes it easy for all to accept and believe the truth." The same Holy Spirit constantly perfects faith by his gifts, so that Revelation may be more and more profoundly understood.*

God could not say: *"Be perfect as your Heavenly Father is perfect"* – unless His Will and grace made it possible to avoid sin and do good, to love – according to His Will. And God has now revealed to us His desire that we go further than accepting His grace in faith; namely, that we accept His Grace of all graces and live in His Divine Will. God has made clear that everyone who wants to live in the Divine Will must desire it and learn about it with sincere effort. The best writings on the Divine Will and on the new era of the Kingdom of the Divine Will are those of Jesus and Mary through Servant of God Luisa Piccarreta. The Grace of All Graces has dawned for mankind. Do you love God enough to accept this grace He so much wants to give you? This grace allows you to fulfill your only purpose: *"It is no longer I who live… it is Christ who lives in me."*

I. PREPARTION FOR LIVING IN THE DIVINE WILL

Recent Saints have been writing about the Grace of all graces – the great gift of the Divine Will. The new Catechism expresses the reality of living in the Divine Will, saying: *"Christ enables us **to live in Him** all that He Himself lived, and **He lives it in us**"* (#521).

St. Hannibal De Francia, an Italian priest, was the great apostle of the *"new and divine holiness"* of the living in the Divine Will. He was the spiritual director of **Servant of God Luisa Piccarreta**, who received years of daily visits and accompanying messages from Jesus and Mary during her life. In 1926, the first 19 volumes of Luisa's spiritual diary were published with the Imprimatur of Archbishop Joseph Leo, with the Nihil Obstat from St. Hannibal Di Francia. In March of 1997, the Tribunal Responsible for Luisa' Cause determined unanimously that Luisa's life was one of heroic virtue and that her mystical experiences were authentic. In 2012, the two theologians assigned to evaluate the writings of Luisa Piccarreta by the Vatican Congregation for the Causes of the Saints gave a positive, that is, a favorable judgment, finding nothing contrary to the Faith in her writings. Also in 2012 in Rome, Fr. Joseph Iannuzzi successfully completed and defended the first doctoral dissertation that analyzed and promoted the mystical writings of Luisa Piccarreta, which was then published with ecclesiastical approbation. The messages of Jesus and Mary in the writings of Luisa Piccarreta are significant to the heavenly messages of our times, revealing much detail about living in the Divine Will, the events of the imminent divine chastisements, when Christ will come to reclaim His Kingdom, and then establish the Kingdom of the Divine Will on earth in the New Era of Peace.

St. Hannibal summarized the divine writings that Luisa received from Jesus. These writings indicated **there were three *fiats*,** or divine interventions in God's Plan in history: the *fiat* of Creation, the *fiat* of Redemption, and the *fiat* of Sanctification. He wrote that the *fiat* of Sanctification is beginning in our times and that it offers us *"a new spirit of a new holiness."*

Entering the Will of God through the Will and Heart of Mary

In anticipation of the New Grace and New Era, several saints were given insights that help to lay the foundation and to help us begin to understand what God has in mind for us to receive. **St. Maximilian Kolbe,** one of the greatest of all Marian saints, wrote:

> *Just as the Immaculata herself belongs to Jesus and to God, so too every soul, through her and in her,* **will belong to Jesus and to God in a much more perfect way** *than would have been possible without her. Such souls will come to love the Sacred Heart of Jesus much better than they would have ever done up to now. Like Mary herself,* **they will come to penetrate into the very depths of love,** *to understand the cross and the Eucharist much better than before. Her divine love will set the world on fire and will consume it; then will* **the 'assumption of souls'** *in love take place.*

He seems to see the coming moment when all persons of good will are to be *"assumed"* into the New Paradise. In Kolbe's writings, one sees the perfect abandonment to the Divine Will, expressed in terms of the Divine Will reigning in Mary. St. Kolbe wrote:

> *The will of Mary Immaculate is so closely united with the will of God that they seem to be* **only one will.** *In fulfilling the will of God we can say without hesitation that we are fulfilling the will of Mary Immaculate.*

On another occasion, he added:

> *Her will is united to, and has identified itself in the closest way, with the Will of God. She lives and operates **only in God and through God**... So we should not be afraid to say that **our only and deepest wish is to do the Immaculate's will as accurately as possible**. By doing this we shall belong to her every day more. And she shall take possession of our whole being. Then, it will no longer be we, but **the Immaculate in us and through us to act** and exercise her influence...*

And remember, She lives always in the Divine Will.

The Most Perfect and Holy Person – Living in the Will of God

St. Faustina Kowalska, has rightly been venerated by millions of Catholics, due to her exceptional cooperation with God's grace. At the root of her holiness was this same grace God now wishes to give to all who truly love Him. Our Lord told St. Faustina:

> *You will **cancel out your will completely** during this retreat, and instead, **my complete Will shall be accomplished in you**. Know that it will cost you much, so write these words on a clean sheet of paper. **'From today on, my will does not exist,'** and then cross out the page and on the other side, write these words, **'From today on, I do the Will of God everywhere, always, and in everything.'***

After receiving this unique grace, St. Faustina wrote:

> *I nourish myself on the Will of God. It is my food... Here is **one word** I need and continually ponder; **it is everything to me**; I*

*live by it and die by it, and it is this... **Holy Will of God.**"* Our Lord also told her: *"Now I know that it is not for the graces or gifts that you love me, but because **My will is dearer to you than life.** That is why I am uniting myself with you so intimately as with no other creature.*

St. Faustina further describes this reality:

*Jesus told me that **the most perfect and holy soul is the one who does the will of the Father**... Oh, if souls would only want to listen to my voice when I am speaking in the depths of their hearts, they would reach the peak of holiness in a short time.*

Jesus said to **Luisa Piccarreta** that this final era of the world, now about to begin, would be the *'Fiat of Sanctification'*, brought about by the Holy Spirit. This unique grace of graces is ascribed to the Holy Spirit, as the Catechism tells us and as Jesus confirmed to **Ven. Conchita** (Concepion Cabrera de Armida) when He said:

*I want to return to the world in My priests... I want to give a mighty impulse to My Church infusing in her, as it were, **a new Pentecost**... May the whole world have recourse to this Holy Spirit since the day of His reign has arrived. **This last stage of the world belongs very specially to [the Holy Spirit]** that He be honored and exalted... I will send Him again clearly manifest in His effects, which will astonish the world and impel the Church to holiness...*

Deifying Us

Our Lord raised up several exemplars of the *"new and divine holiness"*. However, most of these recent Saints are not well known yet. One of the greatest examples is **Bl. Dina Belanger**. Our Lord reportedly told her:

> *Apart from the eternal and perfect happiness that I enjoy in my Father and in myself, **my happiness is to reproduce myself in the souls** that I have created out of love. The more a soul allows me to reproduce myself faithfully in her, the more joy and contentment I find. **The greatest joy a soul can give me is to allow me to raise her up to my Divinity**. Yes, my little Bride, I take immense pleasure **in transforming a soul into myself**, in **deifying it**, in absorbing it wholly into the Divinity.*

> *I want to absorb you, my little Spouse, **to the extent of taking your place**, with all the attributes and with all the perfections of my Divinity... **I want to deify you** in the same way as I united my humanity with my divinity in the Incarnation... **The degree of holiness that I want for you is the infinite plentitude of my own holiness**, it is the holiness of my Father brought about in you through me... for the greater glory of my Father, to give joy to my Heart and for the salvation and sanctification of souls.*

Another example of the *"new and divine"* holiness is **Bl. Elizabeth of the Trinity**, a Carmelite nun who was born in 1880 and died in 1906. Bl. Elizabeth wrote:

> *O consuming fire! Spirit of love! Descend within me and reproduce within me, as it were, an Incarnation of the Word that I may be to Him another humanity wherein He renews His*

mystery! O my Christ, Who I love... I beseech You to clothe me
with Yourself, to identify my soul with all the movements of
*Your own. **Immerse me in Yourself;** possess me wholly;*
***substitute Yourself for me,** that my life may be but a radiance*
of Your own.

Bl. Elizabeth also expressed her desire and intention to help all souls
achieve the special grace she received, which God wants to pour out
upon every person:

In Heaven, I believe that my mission will be to draw souls to
interior recollection, by helping them to renounce self (will) in
order to adhere to God in all simplicity and love; to maintain
*them in that profound interior silence which **allows God to***
imprint Himself upon them and to transform them into
Himself.

This new holiness spoken of by modern mystics is similar to that
promoted by **Servant of God Cora Evans**, an American Catholic lay
woman and mother of the twentieth century who was a mystic and
stigmatist, whose writings have received positive Church recognition.
She was commissioned by Our Lord to write about the devotion of
"The Mystical Humanity of Christ". Her writings call us to embrace
the devotion of a heightened awareness of **the living, indwelling**
Presence of the resurrected Christ in our daily lives, that is a form
of an ongoing spiritual communion with Jesus glorified. This devotion
also draws us to deeper and more frequent Sacramental communion in
the Eucharist and from the Eucharist into this devotion. Cora explains
the Indwelling of Christ as follows: *"Through us He uses our bodies*

to accomplish His works of mercy and love. We are His holy dwelling places." We become one with Christ and Christ with us. And in this, we become His other resurrected humanity on earth in the present time and place. Yes, Christ continues His work in us and through us. How marvelous! We become the mystical Humanity of Christ!

God Takes Possession of Us

Ven. Concepcion (Concepion Cabrera de Armida) was a married woman with six children. Her husband died after only 17 years of marriage. "Conchita" as she was known, received many mystical experiences from Jesus, which have received positive Church recognition. Our Lord teaches us about this new unparalleled grace through His conversations with her. When Conchita first received the grace, she thought she had received Our Lord as if in Holy Communion. Our Lord instructed her otherwise, saying: *"It is not that way. Today you have received Me in yet another way. **I am taking possession of your heart**... to never again separate Myself from you. Only sin will be able to separate me from you. This is a very great grace that comes to you prepared by My goodness. Humble yourself and be grateful for it."* Our Lord told Ven. Concepcion about the progression into deepest union with Himself, saying:

> *There are many progressive degrees in the transformation. The highest degree on earth corresponds to a transformation of the creature not only in its manner of thinking and acting which **becomes divine**, but which, in a certain sense, **causes it to disappear and annihilate itself to give place to Me.** This*

degree is the work of the Holy Spirit alone who becomes the soul of this soul and the life of this body.

"The Grace of All Graces"

Conchita then asked the Lord if it was the grace of *"betrothal"* or *"spiritual marriage"*. Our Lord responded: *"It is more, because marriage is a type of union that is more external; to become incarnate is **to live and grow in your soul** without ever leaving; for Me to possess you and for you to possess Me as if in one substance; without your giving life to Me, but rather I giving Myself to your soul in a **compenetration** that you cannot understand; **this is the grace of graces**."*

Throughout her life Conchita grew in the understanding of this grace of graces. Our Lord taught her that it was an actual sharing in the grace given to Mary. Our Lord described it as a *"Mystical Incarnation"*. She described it as follows:

> *This Mystical Incarnation is an imitation of that which was brought about in Mary, but an imitation in the divine sense, through the same Divinity. It is a unitive, transformative, and mutually penetrative grace in which the Most Holy Trinity takes part, for it is a participation in the fruitfulness of the Father that the Holy Spirit achieves in order **to make a Jesus out of the soul**. It is the union of the Word Incarnate with a soul in order **to reproduce the mystery of Christ**, taking a creature as an instrument of sacrifice and immolation, **making**

it a victim in union with Jesus and associating it to the redemption in order to accomplish His plans of love.

Our Lord clearly tells Conchita that many other souls will follow her and become *"golden links"* in a chain to give God the glory He wants through the gift of this grace of graces. He explained this to Conchita:

*You must forget yourself, throw yourself into My arms and offer it all, day and night, **for the salvation and perfection of souls**. You see, you are going to make a chain. Each hour of your life is going to be **a golden link**, being offered with that intention; I wish that it not be broken until your death and this will be your own self-examination...*

*Give yourself to souls as I gave Myself, so you can assimilate yourself with Me. And how did I give Myself? With love, with sacrifice, and without interruption. This is the way I wish your life to be in the future. I want more. **I will choose souls that continue these golden hours** that I wish you to begin without interruption.*

II. LEARNING TO LIVE IN THE DIVINE WILL

One of the greatest ways to grow in holiness and prepare for the new Era is to live according to God's will, to embrace His will in everything. But, there is more, as I have been suggesting. Through mystic Luisa Piccarreta, the Little Daughter of the Divine Will, God is asking us not only to seek and obey His Divine Will, but to live *in* the

Divine Will, which is *"the most beautiful and the brightest among all other sanctities."* Jesus promises: *"If you put yourself at the mercy of my Will, you will* **no longer have concerns for anything**.*"* Living constantly in this way, we will have nothing on our own, but everything will be in common with Jesus. In this, Our Lady's *FIAT* (*"Let it be done to me according to Your Word"*) becomes our constant motto. Our passion is the Divine Will, to *live in* God's Will. This is the fruit of living united to the Two Hearts. As we commit to living our consecrated lives in Jesus and Mary, let us pray to do so by living in the Divine Will.

Living in the Divine Will is the *"new and divine holiness"*. It is important to be faithful and attentive to this Gift, and to learn about and put it into practice. Servant of God Luisa Piccarreta summarizes how to live in the Divine Will by saying that each of us must be focused on *"resigning oneself in everything to the Divine Will, as much in prosperity as in adversity, seeing in all things the Divine Will, the order that the Divine disposition has over all creatures; and that not even one hair can fall from our head if the Lord does not want it."* To understand this, we must distinguish that *"living in the Divine Will"* is not simply like *"doing God's Will"*. Jesus explains:

> **<u>To live in</u> My Will is to reign in it and with it, while <u>to do</u> My Will is to be submitted to My orders**... *To live in My Will is to live with one single Will (the Divine Will Itself, in place of your will, in your soul)... living in My Will is the life that most closely resembles the blessed in Heaven... The distance between the two*

('doing' God's Will vs. 'living' in God's Will) is as far as that of Heaven from earth.

Jesus contrasts the two responses to His Will, saying that while doing His Will involves *"resigning"* and *"conforming"* your will to His Will such there are still two wills involved, living in His Will is to submit to the *"dominion"* of the Divine Will Itself, which then ***"fuses"* the Divine Will with your will**, as one single united Will. God then is free to infuse in your soul great, astonishing, surprising, and unheard of graces in a continuous way.

What makes this new Grace of all graces unique compared to all other means of holiness in the Church until now is that this is the unique, divine, uncreated Gift of grace that actualizes the union of your human will with the Divine Will, as a ***"union of grace"***. This means that your acts are united with the eternal and temporal acts of Jesus Christ Himself, so that your soul comes to do what God does, participating in all His acts – past, present, and future. Yes, this is actually what occurs – as you voluntarily give up your own will (in every sense and manner) to enter the Divine Will, this Grace enables you to act in and with the Will of Christ and to participate in the very divine acts of God Himself. In return, God grants you the Gift of living in the Divine Will, which entails His uniting His divine Nature in a substantial and continuous manner to your human soul and will. This grace disposes you to partake, through virtuous acts, **in God's very Will Itself**, and God's very Will Itself in you. By His Divine Will operating in us, our human will becomes divinized. As Jesus says through Luisa, this is *"the greatest grace"* possible!

While living in the Divine Will is *"a new sanctity"* and even the ***"Sanctity of all sanctities"***, as it forms *"the crown and completion of all other sanctities"*, it is also a hidden sanctity. Those living this Grace appear no different than others striving to live a holy life of grace following God's Will. Thus, you must still strive to fulfill the duties of your state in life, practice charity and the other virtues, frequent the Sacraments, pray, and practice mortifications. You must still aspire to growing in holiness and progress through the three stages of the spiritual life (purgative, illuminative, and unitive). And the more acts you do in the Divine Will, the more you enter within God, and thus the more your soul *"generates the life of God's sanctity, love, light, beauty, power, wisdom"* within itself, and reflects these divine attributes to others.

In many ways, the Grace of living in the Divine Will is more a Gift than a virtue, in that God gives it more than it is acquired, and then the Gift itself makes one more disposed to acquire the most heroic and sublime virtues. To bring things to a simple understanding – on our part, all that is needed is our continual cooperation, so that henceforth we are *"regenerated in [His] Will"* and must increasingly *"let ourselves be **inundated by the goods of the Divine Will**"* – with *"inundations of light, of grace, of love, of sanctity, and of happiness"*! No wonder Jesus says through Luisa that this Grace is *"the last, most beautiful and brilliant ornament among all other sanctities"*, even **surpassing that of all other sanctities**, and that *"the value of [His] Divine Will in you is worth more than everything [and] exceeds the whole value of all creatures together."* Jesus says that on earth *"the* *sanctity of Living in [His] Will is identical to the life of the blessed in Heaven"* except that on earth we can give Him *even more pleasure* in our acts because we can still *"merit"* by engaging in sacrifices of love and enduring sufferings for His glory. This is why the coming Kingdom of the Divine Will will be *"the most beautiful, the most holy, and the **perfect echo** of the Celestial Country (Heaven)."*

Preparing for the Coming Kingdom of the Divine Will

Seeking to complete the glory that man owes to God from the beginning of creation, but which has been lacking since the Fall, those living in the Divine Will will eventually bring about the Kingdom of the Divine Will where in the Era of Peace all humanity will live in His Will on earth as it is in Heaven. About this, Jesus said: *"To reestablish the Kingdom of my Will on earth (as it was with Adam before the Fall), there must be sufficient acts by creatures to keep my Kingdom from remaining suspended and enable It to descend and to take form... Then, if, in truth, the established number has been completed, you can obtain"* the New Kingdom on earth. Jesus also asks us to pray insistently so as to draw down the Eternal Will from Heaven; and with acts of love done in the Divine Will to *"tie"* it to the earth in order that it will reign in the midst of creatures.

It is most important to know that just one act done in the Divine Will is **worth more than the worth of everything in the universe**. What a great mystery to comprehend!

CHAPTER 6

Jesus Will Establish a New Era –
The Second Coming and the
Kingdom of the Divine Will on Earth

Jesus said to his disciples:
For just as lightning flashes
and lights up the sky from one side to the other,
so will the Son of Man be in his day...
As it was in the days of Noah,
so it will be in the days of the Son of Man;
they were eating and drinking,
marrying and giving in marriage up to the day
that Noah entered the ark,
and the flood came and destroyed them all.
Similarly, as it was in the days of Lot:
they were eating, drinking, buying,
selling, planting, building;
on the day when Lot left Sodom,
fire and brimstone rained from the sky to destroy them all.
So it will be on the day the Son of Man is revealed...
Whoever seeks to preserve his life will lose it,
but whoever loses it will save it.
Luke 17:24-33

Behold, he is coming *amid the clouds,*
and every eye will see him,

even those who pierced him.
All the peoples of the earth will lament him.
Yes. Amen.
Revelation 1:7

Those from every people, tribe, tongue, and nation
will gaze on their corpses for three and a half days,
and they will not allow their corpses to be buried...
*But **after the three and a half days**,*
a breath of life from God entered [the two witnesses].
Revelation 11:9-11

Then I saw an angel coming down from heaven, holding in his hand
*the key of the bottomless pit and **a great chain**. And he seized the*
dragon, that ancient serpent, who is the Devil and Satan, and bound
*him for **a thousand years**, and threw him into the pit, and shut it and*
sealed it over him, that he should deceive the nations no more.
Revelation 20:1f

The sun will be turned into darkness,
*and the moon into blood before **the great Day of the Lord**.*
*But **whosoever calls upon the name of the Lord shall be saved**.*
Joel 3:4; Matthew 24:29-31; Acts 2:20-21; Revelation 16:10
*And then **they will see the Son of Man***
***coming** in a cloud with power and great glory.*
Luke 21:27

*I saw one like a **Son of man coming**,*
***on the clouds of heaven**...*
His dominion is an everlasting dominion
that shall not be taken away,
his kingship shall not be destroyed.
Daniel 7:13-14

Jesus said to his disciples:
And then they will see 'the Son of Man coming in the clouds'
with great power and glory,
and then he will send out the angels
and gather his elect from the four winds,
from the end of the earth to the end of the sky...

But of that day or hour, no one knows,
neither the angels in heaven, nor the Son, but only the Father.
Mark 13:24-32

For this we declare to you by the word of the Lord, that we who are
*alive, who are left until **the coming of the Lord,***
shall not precede those who have fallen asleep.
For the Lord himself will descend from heaven with a cry of command,
with the archangel's call, and with the sound of the trumpet of God.
And the dead in Christ will rise first;
then we who are alive, who are left, shall be caught up together with
them in the clouds to meet the Lord in the air;
and so we shall always be with the Lord.
1 Thessalonians 4:15-17

*For behold, I create **new heavens and a new earth**;*
and the former things shall not be remembered or come into mind...
I will rejoice in Jerusalem, and be glad in my people;
no more shall be heard in it
the sound of weeping and the cry of distress.
Isaiah 65:17-19

'Behold, God's dwelling is with the human race.
He will dwell with them and they will be his people and God Himself
will always be with them [as their God].
He will wipe every tear from their eyes,
and there shall be no more death or mourning, wailing or pain,
[for] the old order has passed away.'
The one who sat on the throne said,
*'Behold, **I make all things new.'***
Revelation 21:3-4

Nothing accursed will be found anymore.
The throne of God and of the Lamb will be in it,
and his servants will worship Him.
They will look upon His face,
and His name will be on their foreheads.
Revelation 22:3-4

Then comes the end,
when He hands over the kingdom to His God and Father, when He has
destroyed every sovereignty and every authority and power...
In a moment, in the twinkling of an eye, at the last trumpet...
For the trumpet will sound, and the dead will be raised imperishable,
*and **we shall be changed.***
1 Corinthians 15:24,52

I. LUISA PICCARRETA ON THE COMING CHASTISEMENTS

The coming chastisements are necessary, and God will bring good out of them for those who love Him. Society has built a civilization without God, has given itself a morality contrary to His Law, has justified every form of evil and of sin, and has allowed itself to be seduced by materialism, hatred, violence, pleasure and impurity. Satan has indeed seduced all the nations of the earth with hatred, division, injustice, and war. Jesus and Mary explain more why the chastisements are necessary, through mystic Luisa Piccarreta:

The Chastisements Are Necessary

Jesus said: *The chastisements are necessary; they will serve to prepare the ground so that the Kingdom of the Supreme Fiat may form in the midst of the human family. So, many lives, which will be an obstacle to the triumph of my Kingdom, will disappear from the face of the earth, and therefore **many chastisements of destruction** will take place; other [chastisements] will be formed by creatures themselves to destroy one another. Destruction of entire regions, turmoil of nature, earthquakes, wars, places in desolation, cities deserted, entire streets with houses closed, with no people present, and dead people... human bodies mutilated, floods of blood, towns destroyed, churches profaned...*

Entire cities destroyed, rebellions, the withdrawal of grace from the evil, and also from the very religious who are evil, so that those poisons, those wounds which they had inside, might come out... Ah! I can take no more, the sacrileges are enormous; yet, this is still nothing compared to the chastisements that will come!

The great chastisements that Divine Justice has prepared *– how all the elements will put themselves against man;* ***the water, the fire, the wind, the rocks, the mountains, will change into deadly weapons, and strong earthquakes will make many cities and people disappear*** *– and in all nations... And then, the revolutions which will engulf them.*

Now, the Supreme Fiat wants to get out... the chastisements, cities collapsed, destructions – this is nothing other than the strong writhing of its agony... It wants freedom, dominion... ***What disorder in society, My daughter, because My Will does not reign!***

Many Countries Deserve Chastisements

Almost all nations have united in offending God, and have conspired against Him. Jesus told me (Luisa):

Oh! In what a maze will the nations find themselves, to the point that one will become the terror and the massacre of the other, such that they will be unable to get out by themselves. They will do things as though crazy, as though blind, to the point of acting against themselves. And the maze which poor ***Italy*** *is in... How many shocks she will receive! Remember how many years ago I told you that she deserved the chastisement of* ***being invaded by foreign nations*** *- this is the plot that they are hatching against her.*

(Remember Bl. Elena's prophecy about Russia invading Italy!) *How humiliated and annihilated she will remain! She has been too ungrateful with Me. The nations for which I had a predilection,* **Italy and France, are the ones which have denied Me the most;** *they held hands in offending Me. Just chastisement: they will hold hands in being humiliated. They will also be the ones which will wage war more against the Church.*

Man Lives Like a Beast

Man has lost religion. *Religion is ignored by some of the very ones who call themselves religious…* **this is why man lives like a beast – he has lost religion.** *But even sadder times will come for man, because of the blindness in which he has immersed himself… But the blood which I will cause to be shed by every kind of people – secular and religious –* **will revive this holy religion,** *and will water the rest of the people… Here is the necessity for blood to be shed and for churches themselves to be almost destroyed.*

Therefore, see how necessary the chastisements are in these times, and how necessary it is for death to almost destroy this sort of people, *so that the few who will be left may learn… to be humble and obedient. So, let Me do [it];* **do not… oppose my chastising the people.**

A Revolution in the Church

Luisa discusses a vision she received about the Church:

The Church is so full of interior bitterness, and in addition to the interior bitterness, She is about to receive exterior bitternesses. *I saw people starting* **a revolution,** *entering churches, stripping* *altars and burning them, making attempts on the lives of priests, breaking statues... and a thousand other insults and evils. While they were doing this, the Lord was sending* **more scourges** *from Heaven, and many were killed; there seemed to be a general uproar* **against the Church, against the government, and against one another. I saw many priests running away from the Church and turning against the Church to wage war against her.** *(She says this happened because they focused on human and worldly things, which in turn hardened their hearts to divine things.)*

Jesus then speaks about the religious, priests and enemies of the Church: *In the religious, in the clergy, in those who call themselves Catholics,* **My Will not only agonizes,** *but is kept in a state of lethargy, as if It had no life.* **How many pretend to be my children, while they are my fiercest enemies! These false sons are usurpers, self-interested and incredulous; their hearts are bilges of vice.** *These very sons* **will be the first to wage war against the Church – they will try to kill their own Mother!** *Oh! How many of them are already about to come out into the field. Now there is war among governments and countries;* **soon they will make war against the Church, and Her greatest enemies will be Her own children.** *My Heart is lacerated with sorrow. But in spite of all this, I will let this storm pass by, and the face of the earth and the churches be washed by the blood of the same ones who have smeared them and contaminated them. You too,* **unite yourself to my sorrow - pray and be patient in watching this storm pass by.**

Hope

Mary continues through Luisa, saying:

"May all happen for the Triumph of the Divine Will."

Jesus also speaks about why these things must happen:

But how can It (the Kingdom of the Divine Will) ever come to Reign on earth if evils and sins abound so much as to be horrifying? **Only a Divine Power**, *with one of Its Greatest Prodigies, could do it; otherwise* **the Kingdom of the Divine Will** *will be in Heaven, but not on earth.*

And Jesus shows us His Plan:

How can the Kingdom of the Divine Fiat come if the earth abounds with evil, and (thus) **Divine Justice is arming all the elements to destroy man and what serves man**... *Everything you [see] will serve to purify and prepare the human family. The turmoils will serve to reorder, and the destructions to build more beautiful things. I will stir everything* **for the fulfillment of my Divine Will.**

Reason for Chastisements

My daughter, I am not concerned about the cities, the great things of the earth - **I am concerned about souls.** *The cities, the churches and other things, after they have been destroyed, can be rebuilt. Didn't I destroy everything in the Deluge? And wasn't everything redone again? But if souls are lost, it is forever - there is no one who can give them back to Me.* **Ah! I cry for souls.** *They have denied Heaven for the earth, and* **I will destroy the earth; [then] I will make the sanctity of living in my Will reappear [and the sanctity of future generations] will be so high that, like suns, they will eclipse the most beautiful stars of the saints of the past** *generations.* (This is a similar prophecy to St. Louis de Montfort's.) ***This is why I want to purge the earth***: *it is unworthy of these portents of Sanctity [that will come afterwards].*

False Peace

Through mystic Luisa Piccarreta, Jesus says:

The more it seems that the world is apparently at peace *and they sing the praises of peace, the more they hide wars, revolutions and tragic scenes for poor humanity, under that ephemeral and disguised peace. And **the more it seems that they favor my Church**, singing hymns of victories and triumphs, and practices of* union between the State and the Church, ***the nearer is the brawl that they are preparing against Her****. The same was for Me. Up to the moment when they acclaimed Me as King and received Me in triumph, I was able to live in the midst of peoples; but after my triumphant entrance into Jerusalem, they no longer let Me live; and after a few days they shouted at Me: "Crucify Him!", and all taking arms against Me, they made Me die.*

So too the Church, the Mystical Body, will endure her crucifixion.

II. THE KINGDOM OF THE DIVINE WILL ON EARTH

When you see these things happening,
know that the kingdom of God is near*.*
Luke 21:31

*There will be **a resurrection of the flesh**, followed by **a thousand years** in the rebuilt, embellished, and enlarged city of Jerusalem.*
St. Justin Martyr

The Three Days of Darkness and the Defeat of Satan

This new era will begin after the three days of darkness. Several Saints have prophesied about this event, including St. Pio. Visionary **Bl. Anna Maria Taigi**, whose body is incorrupt, prophesied about the heavenly scourge of three days of darkness, when the wrath of God's justice will commence against His enemies, saying:

> *God will send two punishments; one will be in the form of wars, revolutions and other evils; it shall originate on earth. The other will be sent from Heaven. There shall come over the whole earth* ***an intense darkness lasting three days and three nights***. *Nothing can be seen, and the air will be laden with pestilence which will claim mainly, but not only, the enemies of religion. It will be impossible to use any man-made lighting during this darkness, except blessed candles. He, who out of curiosity, opens his window to look out, or leaves his home, will fall dead on the spot. During these three days, people should remain in their homes, pray the Rosary and beg God for mercy.* ***All the enemies of the Church, whether known or unknown, will perish*** *over the whole earth during that universal darkness, with the exception of a few whom God will soon convert. The air shall be infected by demons who will appear under all sorts of hideous forms.*

Our Lady has also prophesied **at La Salette**, saying:

> *[The Antichrist]* ***will be smothered by the breath of the holy Archangel Michael***. *He will fall, and the earth which for* ***three days*** *will be in continual evolutions will open its bosom* ***full of fire***; *he will be plunged for ever with all his own into the eternal*

*chasms of hell. And then **water and fire will purge the earth** and consume all the work of men's pride, and all will be renewed. God will be served and glorified.*

Melanie, visionary of La Salette, in about 1900, presented the broad outline of the aftermath of the Antichrist, saying:

> *There will only be **true peace on earth after the death of the Antichrist**... After the Antichrist, who will fall body and soul into hell, the ground opening in the presence of the thousands of spectators coming from all the parts of the world to be witness to his exaltation (as he had pre-announced) and (his attempted) entrance to heaven, **all will convert**, glorifying the single God of heaven and earth; the Gospel of Jesus-Christ will be preached in all his purity on all the earth. The churches will be re-established; the kings will be the right hand of the Holy See; there will be one Shepherd and only one herd; charity will reign in all peoples' hearts. The world will still last (for) centuries.*

As **Our Lady of Good Success**, Mary also has promised:

> *I, in a marvelous way, **will dethrone the proud and cursed Satan**, trampling him under My feet and fettering him in the infernal abyss. Thus the Church and Country will finally be free of his cruel tyranny... Then, joyful and triumphant, like a tender child, **the Church will be reborn**.*

During this event, Christ will annihilate the enemies of God, and God will punish the Beast and the False Prophet, as Revelation discusses:

Then I saw... **The beast** *was caught and with it* **the false** **prophet** *who had performed in its sight the signs by which he led astray those who had accepted the mark of the beast and those who had worshiped its image.* **The two were thrown alive** **into the fiery pool** *burning with sulfur (Revelation 19:19-20).*

In the final persecution and general chastisement, the good will experience **miraculous protection**. Recall that Our Lady will keep the elect, the children of God, in her Immaculate Heart, and send angels to protect them, led by St. Michael. Some of the elect will offer themselves as **victims**. *"The blood of the martyrs is the seed of the Church,"* as Tertullian wrote. Sorrow saves; sacrifice redeems. For the great victory, a holocaust of the redeemers is needed. By their sacrifices, the earth will be purified. Look to the Cross of Christ! All for the glory of God and for souls! Fight the world, flesh, and devil!

Then God's Angel will cast Satan into the pit, as the Book of Revelation states: *"Then I saw an angel coming down from heaven... And he seized the dragon, that ancient serpent, who is the Devil and Satan, and bound him* **for a thousand years**, *and threw him into the pit, and shut it and sealed it over him, that he should deceive the nations no more [and* **the holy ones shall reign]** **with Christ** *a thousand years."* The great renewal of peace will come after the great persecution. The Church will then be *resurrected* (first resurrection) after the three days of darkness, where she will experience her mystagogia with Christ's spiritual reign in the millennial Era of Peace with the emerging of the Kingdom of the Divine Will on earth.

The Dawn of the Era of Peace and the New Kingdom

As the New Era begins, there will be a new pope. John of the Cleft Rock prophesied in the fourteenth century, saying: *"**But [then] God will raise a holy Pope**, and the Angels will rejoice. Enlightened by God, this man will rebuild almost the whole world through his holiness. He will lead everyone to the true Faith... He will lead all erring sheep back to the fold."*

The prophecy of Bl. Anna Maria Taigi indicates what will happen after Rome falls, and after the Antichrist is dethroned and the three days of darkness has occurred, stating:

> ***After the three days of darkness***, *St. Peter and St. Paul, having come down from Heaven, will preach in the whole world and designate **a new Pope**. A great light will flash from their bodies and will settle upon the cardinal who is to become Pope. Christianity, then, will spread throughout the world. He is the Holy Pontiff, chosen by God to withstand the storm. At the end, he will have the gift of miracles, and his name shall be praised over the whole earth. Whole nations will come back to the Church and **the face of the earth will be renewed. Russia, England, and China will come into the Church.***

And according to Jesus through mystic Luisa Piccarreta: thus will begin the ***"Celestial and Divine Era of Love"***.

The Fulfillment of the 'Our Father' Prayer

God's Plan is to bring to fulfillment the 'Our Father' prayer in the New Era and to restore humanity to its original state, whereby it will come to pass that the Divine Will reigns universally on earth. This is the greatest revelation for our times – that the Spirit will actualize the fulfillment of the 'Our Father' prayer, especially the two petitions: *Thy Kingdom come, Thy Will be done, on earth as it is in Heaven.*

Through **Luisa**, Jesus states about the 'Our Father' and its future fulfillment: *"I formed this prayer in the presence of My heavenly Father, **certain that He would grant Me the Kingdom of My Divine Will on earth... [now] souls must await it with the same certainty** with which they awaited the future Redeemer."* And this divine promise and assurance is to be accomplished not in a distant heavenly reality only, but here on earth in the New Era of Peace. This will cause to occur the fulfillment of God's Plan to renew the Church and transform the face of the earth. This in turn will set all creation free from its slavery to sin and corruption so that it will enjoy the glorious freedom, like it did before the Fall. The sons of God will freely and continuously exercise their free will under the operation of the Divine Will, when they will live *in the divine Indwelling* of God's Being and in His Divine Will. I can see that glorious day – when God *"delivers us from all evil"*; when the great battle is won, the Two Hearts triumph and reign, and the whole world is renewed; when the *"The New Kingdom has come and God's Will is now being done, on earth as it is in Heaven."* And it is almost here! So, let us henceforth pray with ever-greater devotion and hope: *"Our Father Who are in Heaven... Thy Kingdom come, Thy Will be done, on earth as it is in Heaven... [and] deliver us from evil."*

The Church Sees the Coming New Kingdom of the Divine Will

During the beatification of St. Hannibal Di Francia in 1997, John Paul II stated that there is *"new and divine holiness (living in the Divine Will) with which the Holy Spirit wishes to enrich Christians at the dawn of the third millennium, in order to make Christ the heart of the world."* According to Jesus through Luisa, in the coming Kingdom of the Divine Will, everyone will be invited to live in the Divine Will, *"under the force of a new act, of a continued irresistible force, so that they will feel themselves invested with a **new act of sanctity, of radiant beauty, of the refulgent light**... with new strengths and a **new happiness**... and always one after the other **without ever ceasing**... [and all] will have interminable common goods, because one is the Will that has dominated them."* And as soon as they possess one act in the Divine Will, then another will arrive – one of holiness, one of love, one of light, and so on, without ever ceasing.

Christ prayed: *"Thy Kingdom come, Thy Will be done on earth as it is in Heaven."* How can the Son of God make such a request and not have it fulfilled? After the defeat of the Beast and the False Prophet will unfold the full flowering of the new and divine holiness, the Kingdom of the Divine Will. The Church's position of a holy age to come on the renewed earth is not only sound belief, but also has been the teaching of the Church since the very first Fathers of the Church succeeded St. John the Apostle, the last Apostle to die. Our Lord prayed for the Holy Age to come at the Last Supper, saying:

*I pray not only for them, but also for those who will believe in me through their word, so that they **may all be one**, as you,*

Father, are in me and I in you, that they also may be in us, that the world may believe that you sent me. And I have given them the glory you gave me, so that they may be one, as we are one. I in them and you in me, that they may be brought to perfection as one, that the world may know that you sent me, and that you loved them even as you loved me (John 17:20-23).

The Church in her traditional prayer has always believed and requested this truth: *"Come, Holy Spirit, fill the hearts of the faithful and enkindle within them the fire of Thy Love. Send forth Thy Spirit that we may be created and Thou **shall renew the face of the earth**."* The second part of this prayer is nearly identical to Psalm 104:30. Just five verses later, David concludes this Psalm at verse 35: *"May sinners vanish from the earth, and the wicked be no more."* And so it will be.

In the Book of Acts (3:19f), **St. Peter** describes what will happen:

*May the Lord grant you times of refreshment, and send you the Messiah appointed for you, Jesus, whom heaven must receive **until the times of universal restoration** of which God spoke through the mouth of His holy prophets from of old... this is what was spoken through the prophet Joel: 'It will come to pass **in the last days**, God says that I will pour out **a portion of My Spirit upon all flesh**.'"*

St. Paul also describes it, saying: *"A Sabbath rest still remains for the people of God."* And Ezekiel states: *"I will put **My Spirit within you** and make you live by My statutes, careful to observe My decrees."* **St. Augustine**, the great Doctor of the Church, discusses in *The City of*

God that the belief in an era of peace with the Sabbath rest of the saints is *not* objectionable, saying:

> *Those who, on the strength of this passage [of Revelation 20:1-6], have suspected that **the first resurrection is future and bodily**, have been moved, among other things, specially by the number of **a thousand years**, as if it were a fit thing that the saints should thus enjoy **a kind of Sabbath-rest** during that period, a holy leisure after the labors of six thousand years since man was created... (and) there should follow on the completion of six thousand years, as of six days, **a kind of seventh-day Sabbath** in the succeeding **thousand years**; and that it is for this purpose **the saints rise**, viz.; to celebrate the Sabbath. And **this opinion would not be objectionable**, if it were believed that **the joys of the saints** in that Sabbath shall be **spiritual**, and consequent on the presence of God (in the Eucharist and by living in the Divine Will).*

In **the first resurrection**, those who have been cleansed on this earth, through the great purification, will join those who have also been purified in Purgatory to live in the New Paradise with the Saints. Then the new era of the earthly Kingdom will come, as the Fathers confirm:

> *We do confess that **a kingdom is promised to us upon the earth, although before heaven, only in another state of existence; inasmuch as it will be after the (first) resurrection for a thousand years in the divinely-built city of Jerusalem**...*
> *We say that this city has been provided by God*
> *for receiving the saints on their resurrection,*
> *and refreshing them with the abundance*
> *of all really spiritual blessings,*
> *as a recompense for those which we have either despised or lost.*
> Tertullian, *Adversus Marcion*

I and every other orthodox Christian feel certain that
*there will be **a (first) resurrection of the flesh** followed by a thousand*
*years in **a rebuilt, embellished, and enlarged city of Jerusalem**,*
as was announced by the Prophets Ezekiel, Isaiah and others...
A man among us named John, one of Christ's Apostles, received and
*foretold that **the followers of Christ would dwell in Jerusalem for a***
thousand years**, and that **afterwards the universal, everlasting
***(second) resurrection and (last) judgment** would take place.*
St. Justin Martyr, *Dialogue with Trypho*

And Popes have echoed Scripture and the Church Fathers. **Pope Leo XIII** stated: *"It will at length be possible that our many wounds be healed and all justice spring forth again with the hope of restored authority; that the splendors of peace be renewed, and the swords and arms drop from the hand and **when all men shall acknowledge the empire of Christ and willingly obey His word, and every tongue shall confess** that the Lord Jesus is in the Glory of the Father."* **St. Pius X** saw the day of universal peace and the triumph of the Church, saying:

*Oh! when **in every city and village** the law of the Lord is faithfully observed, when respect is shown for sacred things, when the Sacraments are frequented, and the ordinances of Christian life fulfilled, there will certainly be **no more need for us to labor further to see all things restored in Christ**... And then? Then, at last, it will be clear to all that **the Church**, such as it was instituted by Christ, must enjoy full and entire liberty and independence from all foreign dominion... All this, Venerable Brethren, **We believe and expect** with unshakable faith.*

About this, **Pope Pius XI** concurred: *"And they shall hear my voice, and **there shall be one fold and one shepherd**. May God shortly bring* *to fulfillment His prophecy for transforming this consoling vision of the future into a present reality... We pray most fervently, and ask others to pray for this much desired pacification of society."* Seeing the new civilization of love on the horizon, **Paul VI** agreed:

The unity of the world will be. The dignity of the human person shall be recognized not only formally but effectively. The inviolability of life, from the womb to old age... Undue social inequalities will be overcome. The relations between peoples will be peaceful, reasonable and fraternal. Neither selfishness, nor arrogance, nor poverty... [will any longer] prevent the establishment of a true human order, a common good, a new civilization.

Universal Establishment of the Divine Will

*The Church will be renewed and **the face of the earth transformed through a universal abandonment to the Divine Will**...*
The world is exactly at the same stage
when I was about to come upon earth.
All were awaiting a great event, a New Era; as it indeed occurred.
*The same now; since **the great Event is coming –**
the New Era in which the Will of God
will be done on earth as it is in Heaven.*
Our Lord to Luisa Piccarreta

Our Lord tells us through Servant of God Luisa Piccarreta what the era to come will be like, saying:

It will be a time in which a great *grace [will be given] to the creature as to make him return almost to the state of origin; and only then, when I see man just as he came out from Me, will my Work be complete, and I will take my perpetual rest in the last FIAT... The [New Era of the] FIAT - my 'Fiat Voluntas Tua (Let it be done according to Your Will), on earth as it is in Heaven'* – **will be like the rainbow which appeared in the sky after the deluge**, *which, as a rainbow of peace, assured man that the deluge had ceased.* **So will [this] FIAT be.** *As It comes to be known, loving and disinterested souls will come to live in my FIAT. They will be like rainbows – rainbows of peace – which will reconcile Heaven and earth, and dispel the deluge of so many sins which inundate the earth.* *These rainbows of peace* **will have [this] FIAT as their own life;** *therefore* **my 'Fiat Voluntas Tua' will have Its completion in them.** *And just as the [previous] FIAT called Me upon earth to live among men, [this] FIAT* **will call my Will into souls, and It will reign in them 'on earth, as in Heaven.'**

In this Kingdom, a new era, *a new continuous creation,* **will begin for My Will.** *It will put out everything that It had established to give to creatures, had they always done Its Will, and that It had to keep within Itself for many centuries, as though in deposit, to then release them for the good of the children of Its Kingdom.*

In these manifestations of Mine [is] **the echo of Heaven,** *the long chain of love of the Supreme Will, the communion of goods of our Celestial Father, that He wants to give to creatures; and as though* **wanting to put aside everything that has passed in the history of the world, He wants to begin a new era, a new creation,** *as if the new history of Creation were just now beginning. Therefore, let Me do, because whatever I do is of highest importance.*

When the knowledges about My Divine Will have done their course, in view of the great good that they contain – *goods that* *no creature has thought about until now, that the Kingdom of My Will will be* **the outpouring of Heaven,** *the echo of the celestial happiness, the fullness of terrestrial goods – so, in view of this great good, unanimously,* **[the people] will yearn, they will ask that My Kingdom come soon***... Therefore, one will be the echo from one end of the earth to another, one the sigh, [and they will pray]:* **"May the Kingdom of the Supreme Fiat come."**

Then, triumphantly, It will come into the midst of creatures.

[Thus] the Will of God that the Writings of My Divine Will come to light is absolute, and as many incidents as may occur, It will triumph of everything. And even if it should take years and years, It will know how to dispose everything so that Its absolute Will be fulfilled. **The time in which [the Kingdom of the Will of God] will come to light is relative and conditional** *upon when creatures dispose themselves to receive a good so great,* **and upon those who must occupy themselves with being its criers, and make the sacrifice** *so as to bring* **the new era of peace, the new Sun** *that will dispel all the clouds of evils. However, when my love will make arise the Era of my Will...* **those who want to resist the current will run the risk of losing their lives.**

Afterwards, He added: **The whole world is upside down; everyone is waiting for changes, for peace, for new things.** *They even gather to discuss about it, and they are surprised at not being able to conclude anything and come up with serious decisions. So, true peace does not arise, and everything comes up to words, but no facts. And they hope that more conferences may serve to make* *serious decisions, but they wait in vain. In the meantime, in this waiting, they are all fearful, and some get ready for new wars, some hope for new conquests. But with this, peoples are impoverished and are stripped alive; and while* **they are waiting, tired of the sad era, which, dark and bloody, enwraps them, they wait and hope for a New Era of peace and of light**...

The world is exactly at the same stage when I was about to come upon earth. All were awaiting a great event, a New Era; *as it indeed occurred. The same now; since the great Event is coming –* **the New Era in which the Will of God will be done on earth as it is in Heaven – everyone is waiting for this new Era,** *being tired of the present one, but not knowing what this novelty, this change is, just as they did not know it when I came upon earth. This wait is* **a sure sign** *that the Hour is near. But* **the most certain sign [that this renewal is near] is that I am manifesting what I want to do [through Luisa]**; *and turning to a soul, just as I turned to my Mama in descending from Heaven to earth, I communicate to her my Will and the goods and effects It contains, in order to give It as gift to all humanity.*

Jesus says to Luisa: *My daughter, I repeat it to you –* **do not look at the earth. Let them do what they want. They want to make war – so be it**; *when they get tired, I too will make my war. Their tiredness in evil, their disenchantments, the disillusions, the losses suffered, will dispose them to receive my war.* **My war will be war of love.** *My Will will descend from Heaven into their midst. All of your acts and those of others done in my Volition will wage war on* *the creatures – **but not a war of blood; they will wage war with weapons of love, giving them gifts, graces and peace.** They will give such surprising things as to astonish the ungrateful man. This Will of Mine, militia of Heaven, will confuse man **with Divine weapons**; it will overwhelm him, and will give him the light in order to see – not evil, but the gifts and the riches with which I want to enrich him. **The acts done in my Will,** carrying the Creative Power within themselves, **will be the new salvation of man**; and descending from Heaven, they will bring all goods upon earth. They **will bring the New Era**, and the triumph over human iniquity. Therefore, **multiply your acts in my Will [now] to form the weapons, the gifts, the graces**, so as to be able to descend into the midst of creatures **and wage the war of love on them.***

*... **And when [the Father] sees them almost lost, he [will go] into their midst** to make them richer; he [will offer] remedies for their wounds, and [bring] peace and happiness to all. Now, conquered by so much love, [His] children will bind themselves to their father with a lasting peace, and will love him.*

*Everyone is waiting for this new Era... Peoples – wait and hope for [this] New Era of peace and of light... **the great Event is coming – the New Era in which the Will of God will be done on earth as it is in Heaven.***

What will the New Kingdom be like, when *"the Will of Heaven is one with the earth"*? Through Luisa, Jesus says it will bring more than just peace and salvation for souls; it will bring *"**divine sanctity** in creatures [and] **liberation from all spiritual and bodily evils**, while* *transporting the earth in Heaven in order to make descend Heaven in earth. Therefore asking for the kingdom of my Divine Will is **the greatest thing** – most perfect, most holy."*

The Two Hearts in the Second Coming and the New Era

In His Second Coming, Christ will come to **judge the living and the dead and to establish His Kingdom** in the world, and all through His Mother's Immaculate Heart. The incorrupt Ven. Mary of Agreda spoke about Mary's role concerning the great renewal to come, saying:

*It was revealed to me that **through the intercession of the Mother of God, all heresies will disappear**. This victory over heresies has been reserved by Christ for His Blessed... **Before the Second Coming of Christ, Mary must, more than ever, shine** in mercy, might, and grace in order to bring unbelievers into the Catholic Faith. **The powers of Mary in the last times** over the demons will be very conspicuous. **Mary will extend the Reign of Christ over the heathens** and Muslims, and it will be a **time of great joy** when Mary, as Mistress and Queen of Hearts, is enthroned.*

St. Bernadette spoke a prophecy of our time, saying: *"The Virgin has told me that when the Twentieth Century passes away... **A new Age of Faith** will dawn around the world... There will follow a century of peace and joy as all the nations of the earth lay down their swords and shields. Great prosperity will follow... Millions will return to Christ... The Twenty-First Century will come to be known as the Second Golden Age of Mankind."* Through Mary, the Church will enter **the New Era** of Obedience and Love, of the great universal *Fiat*. It will be a universal reign of grace, beauty, harmony, communion, holiness, justice, and peace! Through Mary, Jesus will reign in hearts, in souls, in individuals, in families, and in all society!

The new Era of Peace will begin with **a new earthly spiritual reign of Christ**. Jesus will *not* be visible in the human flesh, but will gloriously reign anew in our hearts in the Divine Will and, in a most powerful way, by means of the Eucharist. This is **not** related to **the heresy of Millenarianism**, which is the condemned position that Jesus Christ would come down to earth in the flesh (in His *visible* glorified human form) and reign as an earthly king with His Saints for a literal one thousand years before the end of the world. Instead, Christ's New Reign is a spiritual *"reign"* whereby He will bring His Kingdom, the new Jerusalem, to this world in a new way, and He will spiritually manifest Himself to His renewed Church and to His people by the special outpouring of His Spirit through a universal transformation in the hearts and lives of all. Then, all creation will live a fulfilled life in the new terrestrial paradise full of love, joy, peace, and harmony.

Summary of the New Reign of Christ and Universal Restoration

As the new Era of Peace begins with the New Reign of Christ (Revelation 19) when, after the earth is purified with fire and the wicked perish (in the 3 days of darkness), He will send an angel to bind Satan (and his fallen angels) with a great chain (restraint) and throw him into the abyss for '1000 years', removing him from the earth, shutting the door and locking it (from within) and sealing it (from without) to keep him from deceiving the nations anymore. Satan will be removed during the millennium of peace. **The triumph, glory, and honor of the Catholic Church will be established in an instant.** God will be reconciled with mankind in the glorious life of the New Kingdom, the New Era, and the New Beginning.

Jesus will then establish *"His messianic kingdom… to bring all men the definitive order of justice, love, and peace"* (Catechism 671), and He will bring about *"**the first resurrection**"* of the righteous who *"shall reign with him a thousand years"* (Revelation 20:6). Then, as Isaiah states, *"He shall judge between the nations, and set terms for many peoples. They shall beat their swords into plowshares and their spears into pruning hooks. One nation shall not raise the sword against another, nor shall they train for war again"* (2:4)… *And he who dies at 100 will be thought a mere youth… **the wolf and the lamb will feed together**, and the lion eat hay like the ox"* (Isaiah 65:20,25). *"To the victor [He] will give the right to eat from the tree of life that is in the garden of God"* (Revelation 2:7), bestowing Love and Peace.

While Jesus will never reveal to us the date of His coming back to Earth, we do know from the heavenly messages of our times that He is returning **in His Spirit** in our times, in our generation. After the tribulation ends, the Book of Revelation states that His arrival will be heralded by the trumpets in Heaven and the choirs of angels who will sing in praise to announce this Great Event. And **the New Paradise on Earth** will not mean the world will end. Instead, Christ will come to reign over the New Heavens and the New Earth (Revelation 21:1f), which will have now become one. Then, the world will become one holy family, and we will live an existence in accordance with, and in union with, the Divine Will of the Father. The New Paradise, **the heavenly Jerusalem, will descend from Heaven** as the renewed world without end begins. There is *"no temple in it, for the Lord God Almighty and the Lamb are its temple"* and *"the Lamb is its light"*. *"In this **new universe**, the heavenly Jerusalem, God will have his dwelling among men"* (CCC 1044); and *"God will wipe away every tear from their eyes. There will be no more death, nor sorrow, nor crying; and there will be no more pain, for the former things have passed away."*

This is going to be a time of re-union, as **the first resurrection** of the dead will take place. Those who have been cleansed on this earth, through the purification, will join those who have also been purified in Purgatory – to live in the New Paradise. It will be then that we **will be reunited with our loved ones who died in a state of grace and who will be resurrected from the dead in the New Paradise on earth.** Those alive on the earth at His Coming **will become immortal** (in mystical union with His Glorious Body), and they will live a full and perfect life in body and soul – in the most perfect world, the renewed world without end – in the way it was meant to be from the beginning. **We will still have free will but it will be different, as we will be living in complete union with Jesus, according to the Holy Divine Will of the Father.** And Christ does not want us to fear this Day of His Coming, as it will bring us great happiness, peace and joy.

The coming New Kingdom of God will be great, when the Spirit will enlighten and sanctify the Church anew. Then, **the Divine fire of the Holy Spirit will heal the Church of every malady**, will purify her of every stain and every infidelity, will clothe her again in new beauty, will cover her with His splendor, in such a way that she will be able to find again all her unity and holiness, and will thus give to the world her full, universal, and perfect witness to Jesus. We profess in the Creed: *He will come again in glory to judge the living and the dead, and his kingdom will have no end... We look for the resurrection of the dead, and the life of the world to come.*

At the end of the 1000 years of peace, Satan will be released to deceive (tempt) the nations *"in the final (cosmic) unleashing of evil"*, and Gog and Magog, representing the enemies of Israel who are described in Ezekiel 38 and 39, will follow him. They will try to attack the holy ones, but will be destroyed with fire from Heaven, and the Devil will be thrown in the lake of fire to be tormented forever (Rev 20:7-10). The Catechism states: *"The kingdom will be (ultimately and eternally) fulfilled, then... only by God's victory over **the final unleashing of evil**, which will cause his Bride to **come down from heaven**. [And then] God's triumph over the revolt of evil will take the form of **the Last Judgment** after the final cosmic upheaval of **this passing world**"* (677). At this point, **the *"second resurrection"* will occur**, as the Book of Revelation confirms: *"The rest of the dead did not come to life until the thousand years were over"* (20:5). And the Catechism adds: *"The (final) **resurrection of all the dead**, 'of both the just and the unjust,' will precede **the Last Judgment**"* (1038).

There are actually *two* judgments. In **the particular judgment**, immediately at the end of their lives, each person appears before Christ to render an account *"according to what each one has done"*; where the condemned judge themselves to hell for rejecting the Spirit of love (CCC 679) and the rest are granted the beatific vision in Heaven. Then, in **the Last Judgment** at Christ's **final coming** at the end of the Era of Peace, the Son of Man will separate humanity into **two groups** – the sheep with eternal happiness on His right and the goats with eternal loss on His left. *"The Last Judgment will [then] **reveal [to all] even to its furthest consequences the good each person has done or failed to do** during his earthly life"* (CCC 1039). So, now that the Second Coming and eventual Final Judgment of Christ draws near, those who love Him and recognize His Message must devote their time to **spread** His Word and **pray** for the coming Kingdom and salvation of all their brothers and sisters. The **Catechism** (671) summarizes:

> *Though already present in his Church, **Christ's reign is nevertheless yet to be fulfilled** 'with power and great glory' **by the King's return to earth.** This reign is still under attack by the evil powers, even though they have been defeated definitively by Christ's Passover. Until everything is subject to him, '**until there be realized new heavens and a new earth** in which justice dwells, the pilgrim Church, in her sacraments and institutions, which belong to this present age, carries the mark of this world which will pass, and she herself takes her place among the creatures which **groan and travail** yet and await the revelation of the sons of God.' That is why **Christians pray, above all in the Eucharist, to hasten Christ's return** by saying to him: Marana tha! 'Our Lord, come!'*

CHAPTER 7

Jesus Wants Us to Help
Usher in the New Kingdom –
What to Do Now

*Finally, **draw your strength from the Lord**...*
Put on the armor of God
so that you may be able to stand firm against the tactics of the devil.
For our struggle is... with the principalities, with the powers,
*with the world rulers of **this present darkness**,*
with the evil spirits in the heavens...
*that you may be able to **resist on the evil day** and,*
*having done everything, to **hold your ground**.*
Ephesians 6:10-17

*The two means to save the world are **prayer and sacrifice***
in these last times in which we live.
Lucia of Fatima

Heaven is asking us to help save the world in these times. This chapter will discuss *how* we can do the things God is asking us to do:

1. How to enter the New Ark – the Immaculate Heart of Mary

2. How to begin to live in the Divine Will – with faith

3. How to pray for the New Era & Kingdom – with hope

4. How to spread this urgent heavenly Message – with love

I. HOW TO ENTER THE NEW ARK – THE IMMACULATE HEART OF MARY (AND THE SACRED HEART OF JESUS)

Totus tuus.
I am totally yours, Mary.
St. John Paul II's papal motto,
taken from St. Louis de Montfort

St. Louis Marie de Montfort teaches that Marian Consecration is perfect devotion, which is living always consecrated to Jesus through Mary. John Paul II was a great advocate of this devotion, and he recommended *"the figure of Saint Louis Marie Grignion de Montfort, who proposes consecration to Christ through the hands of Mary, as an effective means for Christians to live faithfully their baptismal commitments."* St. Louis de Montfort explains Marian consecration in his treatise, **True Devotion to Mary**. He says: *"This devotion is **a smooth, short, perfect and sure way** of attaining union with our Lord, in which **Christian perfection** consists."* He explains, as follows:

> As all perfection consists in our being conformed, united and consecrated to Jesus it naturally follows that **the most perfect of all devotions** is that which conforms, unites, and consecrates us most completely to Jesus. Now of all God's creatures Mary is the most conformed to Jesus. It therefore follows that, of all devotions, devotion to her makes for the most effective consecration and conformity to him. **The more one is consecrated to Mary, the more one is consecrated to Jesus.**

That is why perfect consecration to Jesus is but a perfect and complete consecration of oneself to the Blessed Virgin, which is the devotion I teach; or in other words, it is the perfect renewal of the vows and promises of holy baptism.

This devotion consists in giving oneself entirely to Mary in order to belong entirely to Jesus through her. *It requires us to give:*

1. *Our body with its senses and members;*
2. *Our soul with its faculties;*
3. *Our present material possessions and all we shall acquire in the future;*
4. *Our interior and spiritual possessions, that is, our merits, virtues and good actions of the past, the present and the future.*

In other words, ***we give her all that we possess*** *both in our natural life and in our spiritual life* ***as well as everything we shall acquire in the future*** *in the order of nature, of grace, and of glory in heaven. This we do* ***without any reservation****, not even of a penny, a hair, or the smallest good deed. And we give for all eternity without claiming or expecting, in return for our offering and our service, any other reward than the honor of belonging to our Lord through Mary and in Mary, even though our Mother were not – as in fact she always is – the most generous and appreciative of all God's creatures.*

Through this consecration, which should be made only with great docility and solemnity, we completely resign ourselves to Mary's will, to her generosity, and to her protection, placing ourselves henceforth at her disposal. **It is precisely in the complete surrender of our lives to the Blessed Virgin that come the most extraordinary graces.** We become the servant, the voluntary slave, and the absolute property of Mary. Then, we rely upon her for absolutely everything. And besides our life and will, we give Mary our heart.

Through stigmatist **Berthe Petit**, whose writings have Church recognition, Jesus calls us to both a heartfelt consecration and genuine devotion to the Immaculate Heart as well as to His Heart through the heart of His Mother. Jesus says:

> *It is hearts that must be changed.* This will be accomplished only by the Devotion [to the Sorrowful and Immaculate Heart of Mary] proclaimed, explained, preached and recommended everywhere. Recourse to My Mother under the title I wish for her universally, is **the last help I shall give before the end of time**... internal peace and confidence in **My Church will revive through the spread of the Devotion and the Consecration** which I wish in order that the Sorrowful and Immaculate Heart of My Mother, united in all to My Heart, may be loved and glorified. **Deliverance will thus be the work of our two Hearts**...

What is requested is *both* full consecration and true devotion. Berthe was then told that this would thus lead to the *"regeneration"* of the whole world. So, consecration itself is not enough. We must learn to not only be consecrated to Our Lady's heart, but to live this consecration in our daily life. **Our Lady of America** says:

*My children think they have done enough in consecrating themselves to my Immaculate Heart. It is **not enough**. That which I ask for and is most important many have not given me. What I ask, have asked, and will continue to ask is **reformation of life**. There must be sanctification from within. **I will work my miracles of grace only in those who ask for them and empty their souls of the love and attachment to sin and all that is displeasing to my Son.** Souls who cling to sin cannot have their hands free to receive the treasures of grace that I hold out to them.*

The way to practice the Two Hearts Devotion is three-fold:

1. **Attain** an image of the Two Hearts and **enthrone** them in your home (and office, parish, community center). You can order picture sets at www.TwoHeartsPress.com

2. **Consecrate** yourself and family to the Immaculate Heart of Mary and to the Two Hearts by reciting the prayers below. **Consider** making the full 33-day preparation for Marian Consecration as outlined by St. Louis de Montfort. **Renew** these prayers regularly, even daily.

3. **Practice** the devotion by personal prayer directed to the Two Hearts. And **reform** your life. As part of this devotion, Our Lady of Fatima asked *her children* to **offer** little sacrifices every day, saying as we offer them: *"O my Jesus, it is for love of You, in reparation for the offenses committed against the*

Immaculate Heart of Mary, and for the conversion of poor sinners."

We must remember that at the last major Apparition of Fatima, on **October 13, 1917, the Miracle of the Sun** occurred. What **a great miracle**! After a long rainstorm, the skies suddenly cleared and the sun came out. The sun began to move around in the sky, as if dancing, and then it began to crash toward the earth. The people responded with fear, and many thought they were going to die and that the world was coming to an end. But, then the sun stopped and returned to its original place and all were blessed. Immediately afterwards, the ground and the people's clothes were completely dry. Images of Jesus, Mary, and Joseph then appeared in the sun and were seen by all, believers and unbelievers alike. It is interesting to note that only 3 people witnessed the Transfiguration, and an amazing 500 people witnessed Jesus Christ after His Resurrection before His Ascension into Heaven. We believe in their testimony, we rest our faith upon it. We should believe as well in our times when a staggering 70,000 people witnessed the Miracle of the Sun at Fatima in 1917. What a marvelous sight! Yet only a prelude to what will occur in our times! Let us daily pray and renew our consecration to Mary and to the Two Hearts!

Marian Consecration Prayer – *Totus Tuus*

I, (name), a faithless sinner,

renew and ratify today in your hands, O Immaculate Mother,

the vows of my Baptism;

I renounce forever Satan, his pomps and works;

and I give myself entirely to Jesus Christ, the Incarnate Wisdom,

to carry my cross after Him all the days of my life,

and to be more faithful to Him than I have ever been before.

In the presence of all the heavenly court,

I choose you this day for my Mother and Queen.

I deliver and consecrate to you, as your slave,

my body and soul, my goods, both interior and exterior,

and even the value of all my good actions,

past, present, and future;

leaving to you the entire and full right of disposing of me,

and all that belongs to me,

without exception, according to your good pleasure,

for the greater glory of God,

in time and eternity. Amen.

St. Louis Marie de Montfort

Prayer to the Two Hearts

*Hail, most loving Hearts of Jesus and Mary! We venerate You. We love
and honor you. We give and consecrate ourselves to You forever.
Receive us and possess us entirely. Purify, enlighten, and sanctify us so
that we may love You, Jesus with the heart of Mary,
and love you, Mary, with the Heart of Jesus.
O Heart of Jesus, living in Mary and by Mary! O heart of Mary,
living in Jesus and for Jesus! O Heart of Jesus pierced for our sins and
giving us Your Mother on Calvary! O heart of Mary pierced by sorrow
and sharing in the sufferings of your Divine Son for our redemption!
O sacred union of these Two Hearts.
Praise be God, the Father, the Son, and the Holy Spirit. Praise be
the Holy Spirit of God Who united these Two Hearts together! May He
unite our hearts and every heart so that all hearts may live in unity, in
imitation of that sacred unity which exists in these Two Hearts.
Triumph, O Sorrowful and Immaculate Heart of Mary! Reign, O
(Eucharistic and) Most Sacred Heart of Jesus! In our hearts, in our
homes and families, in Your Church, in the lives of the faithful, and in
the hearts of those who as yet know You not, and in all the nations of
the world. Establish in the hearts of all mankind
the sovereign triumph and reign of Your Two Hearts
so that the earth may resound from pole to pole with one cry:*
**"Blessed forever be the (Eucharistic and) Most Sacred Heart of
Jesus and the Sorrowful and Immaculate Heart of Mary!"**
*O dearest St. Joseph, I entrust myself to your honor and give myself to
you that you may always be my father, my protector and my guide on
the way to salvation. Obtain for me a greater purity of heart and a
fervent love of the interior life. After your example, may I do all my
actions for the greater glory of the Triune God in union with the
(Sacred) Heart of Jesus and the Immaculate Heart of Mary.
O Blessed St. Joseph, pray for me that I may share in the peace and
joy of your holy death. Amen.*

Two Hearts Media

II. HOW TO BEGIN TO LIVE IN THE DIVINE WILL (WITH FAITH)

How can you begin to live in the Divine Will? There are a few practical ways to begin living in this Grace of all graces, as follows:

1. Intend to never do your own will any longer
2. Learn about the so many new knowledges of living in the Divine Will (many of which are in this book), and experience *"the joy and happiness that this new knowledge brings"*
3. Desire to live in the Divine Will and pray for it
4. Begin to enter God's Will in all your acts, through the daily First Act and ongoing Current Acts (see about this below)
5. Gradually come to 'possess' God, and God will likewise come to 'possess' your soul and will
6. Grow in the Life of this Gift in your daily life and appreciate it
7. Work to bring God's Kingdom to earth and spread it to others

The Two Acts in the Divine Will

Living in the Divine Will is about a relationship. Christ reveals the Grace and offers it to us. We come to *know* about it, *love* it, and *long* for it. He then both *gives* us the Grace and *forms* in us the life of His Will. Living in the Divine Will is not difficult, once you know its secret. It is as simple as removing the pebble of your own will. Your will alone hinders the flow of the Divine Will. Once removed, you flow in Him and He in you; and you *"will find all His goods at [your] disposal: power, light, assistance and everything [you] desire."* One thing alone is needed: you *"only need to desire it and all is done."* With your desire, God will take over and do all the work. From that point, we don't just live for God, but in Him, in His divinity. *"Abandon everything to find everything in God."* Practically speaking, this is done in two ways daily:

1. The First Act

To live your daily life in the Divine Will, Jesus gave us the Prevenient Act, or the "First Act" to begin your day. Do this once upon rising each day. With the First Act, you set your will in the Divine Will and make a prayer to live and act only in the Divine Will that day. This is your predisposing consent. This can be done by a simple spontaneous prayer on your own, or as part of your Morning Offering, or by following a specific Consecration to the Divine Will Prayer. This is how you begin each day. And by it you enter and renew living in the Divine Will. Then as the day progresses, certain human acts may begin to cloud the presence of the Divine Will in your soul, and act to thus eclipse the First Act. So, a second act, the Current Act, is also needed throughout the day. The Current Act clears away any clouds that may have formed, and should be repeated many times throughout the day.

2. The Current Act

To make a "Current Act", simply repeat the First Act's intention to enter into, or remain in, the Divine Will throughout the day in all your acts. It is good to do this several times a day, especially before doing something important. When you are not able to commit your immediate act consciously at various times for whatever reason, then an attitude of good will is enough as well to remain in the Divine Will throughout the whole day.

Thus, only by willful sin, a deliberate doing of your own will, or a complete neglect does one lose the Life of the Divine Will. While one loses sanctifying grace only through mortal sin, the Life of the Divine Will is a little more delicate. Once lost, to regain the Life of the Divine Will in the soul, simply ask God's forgiveness for your fault or neglect or go to Confession if you had committed a mortal sin (as one must be in a state of grace); and then tell Him that you want to live and act only in His Will again. Immediately, you will be restored and continue in the Divine Will. Otherwise, try also to keep a divine attitude of doing everything for and in Christ. In this, you now live such that in each thing you do (for the rest of your life, except in errors or sin), it is Jesus who does it through you, such that nothing remains *"yours"*; all is now *"ours"* in everything between you and Him.

Now, through these two acts in unison each day, the Lord will change your human acts into divine acts, which will reap divine rewards and help to usher in the Kingdom of the Divine Will. Each act truly contains all the goods that are in Heaven and on earth and acquires the same merits of those of Jesus' humanity while on earth.

Jesus says that both First Acts and Current Acts are necessary to live in the Divine Will, and He explains the importance of both, saying: *"The prevenient act (first act) assists, creates the disposition, and makes room for the current act. The current act preserves and enlarges the disposition of the prevenient act."* Thus, you will now arise and live each day in the Light of the Will of God, in the Grace of all graces. And remember, this great Grace is for everyone, so share the good news!

Making Rounds in the Divine Will

As part of living in the Divine Will, Jesus also explains to Luisa about engaging in what He calls the *"rounds"*. To restore God's rightful claims over all creation, effected by the Fall, Jesus invites us to go throughout all creation in prayer to restore the love and glory of God as the center of all He made and did for humanity in the Creation, thus helping to restore the original order of Creation. Through prayer and the operation of the Trinity, **God assists the soul to *"bilocate"* as it makes its *"rounds"* in creation**. Luisa shows us how to do this by reflecting on the sun, the seas, the plants... as we then impress our prayer of 'love' and 'glory' upon them, for everything He did in Creation, so as to make up for all that the human will had broken (by lack of due 'love') and establish the 'glory' that everyone owes to Him. By doing the rounds, we assist in causing His Will to again descend to earth, as it was before the Fall, and to **return all things to the *"original order"*** they had as God first created them. What a great Gift! What a supreme Glory! What unity of Love!

Jesus also taught Luisa *"a new method"* about how to *enter into* what He did in His earthly Life and His Passion (and what He does now in the Eucharist) in a similar way as the rounds of Creation (through prayer in the Divine Will), so as to teach us, through her, to repeat in our soul His Acts of Redemption and Salvation. To assist us in this more specifically, Jesus dictated to Luisa *"the **internal acts** of*

His humanity" in the book, *The Hours of the Passion of Our Lord Jesus Christ*. Our Lady gave Luisa a similar book related to her own interior life on earth, called *The Virgin Mary in the Kingdom of the Divine Will*. **As we practice making the First Act each day and repeating the Current Acts throughout the day (and begin making the *"rounds"* of Creation and Redemption) we will help to restore the original order of Creation, make *"infinite"* reparation for souls while helping to avert God's justice as co-redeemers, and ultimately contribute to ushering in the Kingdom of the Divine Will on earth!** What unimaginable splendor, what glorious majesty God has given us in the Gift and Life of the Divine Will! Start today!

III. HOW TO PRAY AND PREPARE FOR THE NEW KINGDOM (WITH HOPE)

Begin with the Rosary – in the Family

> *Say the Rosary every day to obtain peace for the world.*
> Our Lady of Fatima

> *The Rosary is THE WEAPON.*
> St. Pio

> *One day, through the Rosary and the Scapular, I will save the world.*
> St. Mary to St. Dominic

Many know of **Bl. Mother Teresa of Calcutta** who founded the Missionaries of Charity to bring Christ to the poorest of the poor, but few know that she was inspired to found the new congregation as *"the call within the call"* due to a mystical experience she received of three visions of Jesus and Mary, at the center of which was **the heavenly call to have families pray the Holy Rosary**. I think it is important to see these visions as Jesus and Mary speaking to you right now, where you are, today. Mother Teresa describes the three visions in her own words, published after her death, saying:

1) *I saw a very big crowd... They called out:* **"Come, come, save us** *– bring us to Jesus."*

2) *I could see great sorrow and suffering in their faces – I heard Our Lady say: "Take care of them – Fear not. **Teach them to say the Rosary – the family Rosary and all will be well**. – Fear not – Jesus and I will be with you and your children."*

3) *Our Lord on the Cross. Our Lady at a little distance from the Cross – and myself as a little child in front of her... Our Lord said – "I have asked you. They have asked you and she, My Mother has asked you. Will you refuse to do this for Me –* **to take care of them, to bring them to Me?***

In 2002, St. John Paul wrote an apostolic letter on the Rosary, saying:

*[The Rosary is] a prayer of and for **the family**... **The family** that prays together stays together... To pray the Rosary for children, and even more, with children, training them from their earliest years to experience this daily 'pause for prayer' **with the family**... is a spiritual aid which should not be underestimated... Why not try it?... May this appeal of mine not go unheard!*

Today, God is calling you to help save yourselves, your families, and the *"great crowd covered in darkness"* by praying the family Rosary. About the **new divine power** of the Rosary, **Lucia of Fatima** said:

*The Most Holy Virgin <u>in these last times in which we live</u> has given **a new efficacy to the recitation of the Rosary** to such an extent that **there is no problem**, no matter how difficult it is, whether temporal or above all spiritual, in the personal life of each one of us, of our families, of the families of the world, or of the religious communities, or even of the life of peoples and nations **that cannot be solved by the Rosary**. There is no problem I tell you, no matter how difficult it is, that we cannot resolve by the prayer of the Holy Rosary. With the Holy Rosary, **we will save ourselves. We will sanctify ourselves. We will console Our Lord and obtain the salvation of many souls**.*

The Blessed Mother gave **fifteen promises** to St. Dominic and Bl. Alan de la Roche **for those who pray the Rosary regularly with devotion**. She says that she promises:

1. signal graces.
2. her special protection and the greatest graces.
3. it will be a powerful armor against hell, destroy vice, decrease sin, and defeat heresies.
4. it will cause virtue and good works to flourish; will obtain for souls the abundant mercy of God; will withdraw the hearts of men from the love of the world and its vanities, and will lift them to the desire of eternal things.
5. you shall not perish.
6. you shall never be conquered by misfortune; shall not perish by an unprovided death; if you be already just, you shall remain in the grace of God and become worthy of eternal life.
7. you shall not die without the Sacraments of the Church.
8. you shall have during your life and at your death the light of God and the plenitude of His graces; at the moment of death you shall participate in the merits of the Saints in paradise.

9. she shall deliver you from purgatory.
10. you shall merit a high degree of glory in Heaven.
11. you shall obtain all you ask of her.
12. you shall be aided by her in your necessities.
13. you shall have for intercessors, the entire celestial court during your life and at the hour of death.
14. you are her sons (and daughters), and brothers (and sisters) of her only Son, Jesus Christ.
15. it is a great sign of predestination (according to its Catholic understanding). Oh, that souls would sanctify themselves by this means, she says.

In the last apparition at Fatima with the Miracle of the Sun, Our Lady appeared as Our Lady of Mt. Carmel, holding the brown Scapular in her outstretched hand. **The Scapular** is the sign of our consecration to Mary's Immaculate Heart. As we wear it with devotion, it should daily remind us of the promise we have made to her. Lucia said: *"Our Lady wants all to wear the Scapular... Yes, **the Rosary and the Scapular are inseparable!**"* To decide not to wear the Scapular or not to pray the Rosary daily is to say *"No"* to Our Mother, who has asked this of *you* with her loving Motherly Heart. **St. Alphonsus Liguori** said: *"Those who say the Rosary daily and wear the Brown Scapular and who do a little more, will go straight to Heaven."* To Maria Esperanza, Mary says: *"I am the Mother of Mount Carmel, who **with my Scapulars** comes to save each one of you... so you may live in accordance with the divine will."* What is most important to take from this book is that Our Lady wants us to enter her Immaculate Heart as the New Ark of our times, and to practice devotion to her Heart by praying the daily Rosary in the family. In cases where not all the family members are willing to gather to pray the Rosary, gather with those who are willing, while being patient with the others, praying for them during the Rosary, occasionally asking them to join you, and moving forward with peace. Even better, organize or join a Rosary prayer group with other families. We need each other to make it in these times! Unity is the key to the God's Kingdom! Mary is Mother of the Family and of Community!

Reparation to the Heart of Mary & the Coming Triumph

Let us understand that God has given us the gift of the devotion to Mary's Sorrowful and Immaculate Heart for these times, so that with it we can save souls, defeat Satan (and the evils of the false prophet, the antichrist, and communism), and help usher in the great victory in this final battle. Jesus is also asking us to atone for the sins and offenses that humanity has caused His Mother. He wants us to affectionately repair the hurts the world has caused our heavenly Mother. On the evening of Thursday, December 10, 1925, after supper, **Sister Lucia of Fatima** received a visit by the Child Jesus and the Virgin Mary in her convent cell.

The Divine Child was the first to speak to Lucia: *"Have pity on the Heart of your most Holy Mother. It is covered with thorns with which ungrateful men pierce it at every moment, and there is no one to remove them with an act of reparation."*

Our Lady of Fatima promised: *"I promise to help at the hour of death with the graces needed for salvation those who, **on the first Saturday of five consecutive months**, go to confession, receive Holy Communion, say five decades of the Rosary and keep me company for* *fifteen minutes while meditating on the mysteries of the Rosary, with the intention of making reparation to my Immaculate Heart."*

Our Lady then said: *"Look... at my Heart, surrounded with thorns with which ungrateful men pierce me at every moment by their blasphemies and ingratitude... Ask, ask again insistently for* **the promulgation of the Communion of Reparation in honor of the Immaculate Heart of Mary on the first Saturdays.**

Jesus continued later saying: *"Many souls begin* **the First Saturdays**, *but few finish them, and those who do complete them do so in order to receive the graces that are promised thereby. It would please Me more if they did Five with fervor and with the intention of making reparation to the Heart of your heavenly Mother, than if they did Fifteen, in a tepid and indifferent manner."*

Lucia received a great vision, which revealed how Russia would be converted, in the chapel of her convent at Tuy, Spain. She explained it as follows:

Suddenly the whole chapel was lit by a supernatural light, and above the altar appeared a cross of light, reaching to the ceiling. In a brighter light on the upper part of the cross, could be seen the face of a man and his body as far as the waist. Upon his breast was a dove of light. Nailed to the cross was the body of another man. A little below the waist I could see a chalice and a large host suspended in the air, on to which drops of blood were falling from the face of Jesus Crucified and from the wound in His side. These drops ran down on to the host and fell into the chalice. Beneath the right arm of the cross was Our Lady and in her hand was her Immaculate Heart. (It was Our Lady of Fatima, with her Immaculate Heart in her left hand, without sword or roses, but with a crown of thorns and flames). Under the left arm of the cross, large letters, as if of crystal clear water which ran down upon the altar, formed these words: 'Grace and Mercy.'

Sr. Lucia continues: *"I understood that it was **the Mystery of the Most Holy Trinity** which was shown to me, and I received lights about this mystery which I am not permitted to reveal. Our Lady then said to me: '**The moment has come in which God asks the Holy Father, in union with all the bishops of the world, to make the consecration of Russia to my Immaculate Heart, promising to save it by this means.'"***

On March 19, 1939 Lucia wrote the message of Jesus as follows: *"**The time is coming when the rigor of My justice will punish the crimes of diverse nations.** Some of them will be annihilated. At last the severity of My justice will fall severely on those who want to destroy My reign in souls. **Whether the world has war or peace depends on the practice of this devotion**, along with the consecration to the Immaculate Heart of Mary. This is why I desire its propagation so ardently, especially because this is also the will of our dear Mother in Heaven."*

On June 20, 1939 Lucia again wrote: *"Our Lady promised to delay the scourge of war, if this devotion was propagated and practiced. We see that She will obtain remission of this chastisement to the extent that efforts are made to propagate this devotion; but **I fear that** we cannot do any more than we are doing and that **God, being*** *displeased, will pull back the arm of His mercy and let the world be ravaged by this chastisement which will be unlike any other in the past, horrible, horrible.* " Unfortunately, as people did not respond, WWII broke out two months later. We may wonder today: what is to come in our time, far worse than in the last century, if we do not listen and heed these heavenly messages while there is still time?

To fulfill Mary's request of communion of reparation, you must do four things on the First Saturday of five consecutive months:

1. Receive Jesus in Holy Communion (If this is not possible on Saturday, then the Sunday following)

2. Receive the sacrament of Reconciliation (or a week before or a week after)

3. Say a Rosary (5 decades)

4. Keep Our Lady company for fifteen minutes while meditating on the mysteries of the Rosary

Your motive for doing these must be to make reparation for sins and offenses against Mary's Immaculate Heart, for the five offenses she suffers (and hence, it is a devotion of FIVE first Saturdays):

1) For blasphemes against her Immaculate Conception

2) For blasphemes against her perpetual virginity (before, during, and after birth)

3) For blasphemes against her Divine Maternity of Jesus and against her spiritual motherhood of all Christians

4) For the neglect of imbuing children with a knowledge and love of the Immaculate Mother of God

5) For offense against statues and images of Mary

Our Lady promised that all who make the Five First Saturdays Devotion will have all the graces necessary for salvation provided to them at the hour of death and that through this devotion, with the Consecration of Russia, she would grant peace to the world. Salvation for souls, peace for the world... this is a great devotion indeed!

Holy Mass and Eucharistic Adoration

The Church teaches that Mass is the source, summit and font of the whole Christian life. This means that if we did nothing today but attend and actively participate in Mass, with proper disposition, then we could do nothing greater or more efficacious for the glory of God and the good of souls. The Catechism (#1389) even recommends the faithful to receive the Eucharist daily, saying: *"The Church obliges the faithful to take part in the Divine Liturgy on Sundays and feast days... the Church strongly encourages the faithful to receive the holy Eucharist on Sundays and feast days, or more often still, even **daily**."* Let the Mass give you your daily divine Food and your daily peace. Make holy Mass the center of your daily life now, as the Eucharist will be the center later for the entire world and every person in the Kingdom of the Divine Will. Let Mass be your life – the central, pivotal act of every day of your earthly life!

At weekly **Adoration of the Blessed Sacrament**, *special graces are being granted.* We must learn to **pray until prayer becomes a great joy** for us, and as St. Paul says, pray unceasingly. The saints tell us the great secret of all secrets about the great gift of all gifts:

John Paul II: *YOU have great need for Eucharistic Adoration!*

Pope Paul VI: *In the course of the day, the faithful should not omit visiting the Blessed Sacrament.*

St. Alphonsus Liguori: *Of all devotions, that of adoring Jesus in the Blessed Sacrament is the greatest after the sacraments, the one dearest to God and the most helpful to us.*

Bl. Mother Teresa: *The time we spend with Jesus in Eucharistic Adoration is the best time we can spend on earth.*

Our Lord revealed to St. Gertrude: *Each time (we go to Eucharistic Adoration) raises our place in Heaven forever.*

St. John Vianney: *In Heaven we will consider these moments with the Lord (in the Eucharist) as the happiest of our earthly lives.*

John Paul II: *The worship of the Eucharist is of inestimable value.*

John Paul II: *I hope that ... perpetual adoration, with permanent exposition of the Blessed Sacrament, will continue into the future. Specifically, I hope... in **the establishment of perpetual Eucharistic Adoration in all parishes and Christian communities throughout the world**.*

With the Eucharist at the center of our daily lives, we will live lives of great joy and holiness. **St. Faustina** wrote before she died in the 1930's: *"All the good that is in me is due to Holy Communion ...I feel this holy fire has transformed me completely... O Lord, my heart is a temple in which You dwell continually."* And as a result of the continual abandonment of her human will to the Divine Will, St. Faustina received the grace of *preserving the Sacred Species in her body from one Communion to the next.* Let this be our goal as well.

Through **St. Margaret Mary**'s visions, **Jesus asks us for** acts of reparation dedicated to His Sacred Heart, for **frequent Eucharistic Communion, and** the keeping of **a weekly Holy Hour, particularly on Thursday nights**, to soothe the heartache He felt when His apostles deserted Him in Gethsemane on Holy Thursday. He asks us to make up for others' ingratitude, by accepting any mortification or humiliation as a token of His love. Make a weekly Holy Hour!

Practicing Devotion to the Sacred Heart to Help Save the World

Let us understand that God has given us the gift of the devotion to Jesus' Eucharistic and Sacred Heart for these times, so that with it we can bring His mercy to sinners, build the Kingdom of God, and prepare the world for His Second Coming. **Our Lord** gave the following **twelve promises** to those who venerate His Sacred Heart Image and adore His Heart in the Eucharist. He will:

1. give you all the graces necessary in your state of life.

2. give peace in your families and will unite them.

3. console you in all your troubles.

4. be your refuge during life and above all in death.

5. bestow the blessings of Heaven on all your enterprises.

6. give sinners the infinite ocean of mercy from His Heart.

7. grant tepid souls fervency.

8. grant fervent souls great perfection.

9. bless those places wherein the image of His Heart shall be exposed and honored and will imprint His love on the hearts

of those who would wear this image on their person (like on the Scapular), and destroy in us all disordered movements.

10. give to priests who are animated by a tender devotion to His Divine Heart the gift of touching the most hardened hearts.

11. have our names written in His Heart, never to be effaced.

12. **First Friday Devotion**: He promises you in the excessive mercy of His Heart that He will grant to all those who (worthily) receive Holy Communion on the First Friday of *nine* consecutive months the grace of final repentance, will not die in His disgrace, nor without receiving the Sacraments; His Heart being your safe refuge in that last moment.

Pope Pius XII stated that devotion to the Sacred Heart of Jesus is *"the foundation on which to build **the kingdom of God** in the hearts of individuals, families, and nations."* We need to honor His Image, as well as other sacramentals including crucifixes, Holy Bibles, rosary beads, religious medals, scapulars, and Benedictine Crosses.

Sin seems to dominate the whole world today. But, there is reason to hope. God has given us a secret weapon to combat sin, to replace sin and death with His mercy, which conquers all. Jesus is calling us to pray by calling out to the Eternal Father and offering Him Jesus' Passion and Redemption in atonement for our sins and the sins of the whole world. To help us to save the world today, Jesus has given us the **Chaplet of Divine Mercy through St. Faustina**. He said to St. Faustina:

> ***Say unceasingly this chaplet** that I have taught you. Anyone who says it will receive great Mercy at the hour of death.*

Priests will recommend it to sinners as the last hope. Even the most hardened sinner, if he recites this Chaplet even once, will receive grace from My Infinite Mercy. I want the whole world to know My Infinite Mercy. I want to give unimaginable graces to those who trust in My Mercy...

...When they say this Chaplet in the presence of the dying, I will stand between My Father and the dying person not as the just judge but as the Merciful Savior.

Pray the Chaplet often. Say always: ***"Jesus, I trust in You."*** Stand up and protect yourselves and your families using this prayer. Even more, God wants you to use this prayer as a prayer of reparation to save the whole world! Jesus said to St. Faustina: By this devotion, ***"you will prepare the world for My final coming."***

New Devotion to St. Joseph – Patron of the Church, the Family, and Chastity

St. Joseph too will come with the Holy Child
to bring peace to the world.
Our Lady of Fatima

God wishes me to be honored in union with Jesus and Mary
to obtain peace among men and nations...
The Divine Trinity has placed into our keeping
the peace of the world.
St. Joseph through the apparitions of Our Lady of America

In the apparitions of Our Lady of America, St. Joseph spoke to visionary Sr. Mildred, giving great insights to bring countless souls to a new way of life, that of honoring his heart, saying:

My spiritual fatherhood extends to all God's children. I am the protector of the Church and the home, as I was the protector of Christ and His Mother while I lived upon earth. Jesus and Mary desire that my pure heart, so long hidden and unknown, be now honored in a special way. *I desire souls to come to my heart that they may learn true union with the Divine Will. The Holy Trinity desires thus to honor me* that in my unique fatherhood *all fatherhood* might be blessed. So *the head of the family must be loved, obeyed, and respected, and in return be a true father and protector to those under his care.* Receive my blessing. May Jesus and Mary through my hands bestow upon you eternal peace.

And at the final apparition of Fatima (1917), just after the Miracle of the Sun, St. Joseph with the Child Jesus and Our Lady robed in white with a blue mantle, appeared beside the sun. St. Joseph and the Child Jesus then blessed the world, for they traced the Sign of the Cross with their hands. All fathers should bless their family members regularly.

Renewed devotion to St. Joseph has also become more of a focus for the Church in recent years. In 2012, the Church officially added an invocation to St. Joseph in the Eucharistic Prayers, just after the invocation to Mary. The papal decree stated that the reason for this new invocation in the Consecration is that the faithful in the Catholic Church have always shown continuous devotion to St. Joseph and have always solemnly honored St. Joseph's memory as the most chaste spouse of the Mother of God and as the heavenly Patron of the Universal Church. Joseph is an important intercessor in these times!

Prayer to St. Joseph

O St. Joseph, whose protection is so great, so strong, so prompt before the Throne of God, I place in you all my interests and desires. O St. Joseph, do assist me by your powerful intercession and obtain for me from your Divine Son all spiritual blessings through Jesus Christ, Our Lord; so that, having engaged here below your Heavenly power, I may offer my thanksgiving and homage to the most loving of fathers. O St. Joseph, I never weary contemplating you and Jesus asleep in your arms. I dare not approach while He reposes near your heart. Press Him in my name and kiss His fine Head for me, and ask Him to return the Kiss when I draw my dying breath. St. Joseph, Patron of departing souls, pray for us. Amen.

Say this prayer for nine consecutive mornings for anything you may desire. It has seldom been known to fail. This prayer was found in the fiftieth year of Our Lord Jesus Christ. In 1505, the Pope sent it to Emperor Charles when he was going into battle. Whosoever reads this prayer or hears it or carries it, will never die a sudden death, nor be drowned, nor will poison take effect on them. They will not fall into the hands of the enemy nor be burned in any fire, nor will they be defeated in battle. Make this prayer known everywhere.

Imprimatur:
Most Rev. George W. Ahr
Bishop of Trenton

So, let's summarize God's Plan for our times: **Consecrated** to the Immaculate Heart of Mary, praying the Rosary (with the First Saturday devotion), we will defeat Satan; **Trusting** in the Eucharistic

Heart of Jesus, praying the Chaplet of Divine Mercy (with the First Friday devotion), we will save the world; being **United** to the Two Hearts as much as Joseph is; and all **Living** in the Divine Will.

Nothing Will Be Impossible for You with Fasting

Pray, fast, and make sacrifices
for your sins and for the sins of all sinners and unbelievers.
Our Lady of Fatima

Fasting has a long tradition in Church practice and life. Christ fasted. He spoke of the power of fasting, saying: *"Nothing will be impossible for you... by prayer and fasting"* (Matthew 2:20-21). The Apostles fasted (Acts 13:2-3, 14:21-3). Fasting is found in the Old Testament (Judith 4:9, 8:5-6; Tobit 12:8; Esther 4:16; Jonah 3:5; 2 Maccabees 13:12) as well. Moses fasted before receiving the Ten Commandments. Elijah fasted while he traveled to Mount Horeb to commune with God. Daniel fasted for three weeks when he received a vision from God warning about a great war. The Bible shows us that fasting is for repentance, atonement, and penance. We fast to show that we are determined to avoid committing evil, and we fast when there is a threat of calamity to implore God's mercy and aid. Devout Jews fasted twice a week (Luke 18:12). The *Didache* (from the 1st century) recommends the Christian faithful to fast on Wednesdays and Fridays. According to tradition, Wednesday is the day Judas made the deal to betray Jesus and Friday is the day of the Passion. Today, God is calling us back to this most important biblical practice.

Fasting empowers one to be chaste and pure. Fasting helps us to overcome our passions, control our sinful inclinations, and to grow in temperance. St. Benedict says to love two things in the spiritual life: *"To love fasting!"* and *"To love chastity!"* Cardinal Ratzinger (Benedict XVI) agrees, saying: *"Sexuality and nutrition belong to the fundamental elements of human corporality: a decreasing understanding of chastity is taking place simultaneously with a decreased understanding of fasting... [Whereas] Chastity and occasional renunciation of food witness [to a renewed focus on] eternal life."* Besides, when one becomes skilled in the denial of food to satisfy the body, one will more easily be able to avoid un-chastity of the eyes or disordinate desires to satisfy the flesh. Fasting is more than a means of developing self-control. Fasting should also be linked to our concern for those who are forced to fast by their poverty. What do we "fast" from? We fast...

+ From Sin: Renounce that which hinders you from being closer to Jesus.

+ From Food: Eat only bread and water, especially on Wednesdays and Fridays

Fasting can be difficult, and in our western culture; we often have a self-induced mental roadblock to the idea of fasting. We should **pray for the gift of fasting**. The best way to fast is strictly on bread and water (which may include fruit) on Wednesdays and Fridays (except major feast days) as penance for the salvation of souls. Fasting should include limiting television and excessive entertainments, for through the internet and the television, a subtle and diabolical tactic of seduction and corruption has found its way into many families. John Paul II wrote on the powerful effects of the union of prayer with fasting, admonishing: *"Let us pray and fast so that the power from on high will break down the walls of lies and deceit... [and instead, build] the civilization of love."*

What is most important to know about **fasting** is that it **is essential to the heavenly Message of our times.** God wants you to fast, in whatever way you are able. We must trust these heavenly admonitions and respond with enthusiasm. Souls are at stake. Even if you can fast for half of the day, or most of the day, each additional hour of fasting into the day will produce so much the more abundant fruit and graces. It often helps to fast for those in need as well, as adding love to your fasting will help to motivate you. But, what is most important is that you fast, beginning anew today!

Our Lady Gives Us God's Perspective on Chastity & Purity

Our Lady at Fatima spoke about fashions which *"will be"* introduced that *"will offend"* the Lord greatly. Ten year old Jacinta lay dying in a hospital bed in Lisbon, Portugal in 1920 when Our Lady said to her: *"Certain fashions will be introduced which will offend Our Divine Lord very much. Those who serve God ought not to follow these fashions."* Then Our Lady revealed to Jacinta: ***"The sins that lead most souls to hell are the sins of the flesh."*** The **Catechism** teaches: *"Modesty means refusing to unveil what should remain hidden. Modesty is decency. It inspires one's choice of clothing"* (#2522). Through the Church-recognized apparitions of **Our Lady of America,**

Mary says: *"I am Our Lady of America. I desire that my children honor me, especially by the **purity** of their lives."* This means that we must strive to foster and live the virtues of purity and chastity, with self-control, while upholding the dignity of all human life, especially in practical ways that include avoiding the sins of lust, fornication, adultery, pornography, contraception, abortion, homosexual acts, masturbation, immodesty of dress, and unchastity of the eyes. In today's culture, chastity and purity are increasing only possible with frequent and regular Confession. So, commit to go to **monthly Confession** – as a remedy against the sins of the flesh and other sins. *For where sin abounds, grace abounds all the more* (Romans 5:21).

So, God is telling us that He wants us to do 4 things to help restore chastity: to fast, to frequent confession, to go to St. Joseph, and to ask Our Lady of America for help. But, for you and me, it is more than that, isn't it? It is not enough for us to strive to be faithful and morally upright ourselves; not in this culture, in this present darkness; we are being called by Jesus and His Mother to more; you and I are being called to pray, sacrifice, and even offer our lives for those who cannot, due to sin and addiction, be faithful and chaste on their own. We need to help those in this world today, and there are many of them, who cannot help themselves. Are you ready; are you willing? Then let's get to it! Offer your life to the Lord for souls! Through Maria Esperanza, Mary says: *"The more you suffer, the closer to you We (Jesus and Mary) will be, soothing, healing the wounds of your hearts, to continue to live with the responsibility of **being redeemers of this time, and saviors in hope** for the great eternity!... Be courageous!"*

IV. HOW TO SPREAD THIS URGENT HEAVENLY MESSAGE (WITH LOVE)

And have YOU spread through the world
what our heavenly Mother requested of you?
Our Lady of Fatima

I wish to share about the conditional aspect of the times we are in concerning the events to come, about how all this is to come depends on us. This book has sought to discuss the Good News of the prophecies of the Saints and Popes and the revelations of God to His people concerning the times we live in today. We now have the mission to share this 'good news' with others and to share our hope. **Our mission** is: *to be consecrated to Mary, the New Ark; to begin living in the Divine Will; to accept the Kingdom of divine peace now; and then to spread this heavenly Message of hope to others.* Each of us hears Jesus speaking to us about our new mission in the Two Hearts, as He says through **St. Faustina**: *"Tell the whole world!"* Thus, dear reader, Jesus and Our Lady are calling *you* to do **two things – to fully live and urgently spread** this heavenly Message! Respond now to live and spread this biblical and heavenly Message of our times! Think about it – what is more important than this?! *You* have been called!

Apostles of Love and Truth – *"The Apostolate of Apostolates"*

In these times, we are being called to be authentic living witnesses of faith, hope, and love. We are being asked to be witnesses (martyrs) of love. Some may be called to a white martyrdom of internal suffering and faithful witness of Christ and to the Faith, while others may volunteer and be called to a red martyrdom of physical suffering and possibly death for the truth of Christ. The grace of the Lord will be sufficient for us and the Lord will never give us more than we can handle. Our merits will be in the intention of love, in the Divine Will, for the glory of God, and the salvation and sanctification of souls; and we shall be filled with the joy of the Spirit!

Our Lord wants to begin the restoration of His Peace *now*, in this initial phase *through you*, through *your* life of holiness and self-giving, through your faithful vocation and fruitful apostolate, **making the Message in this book your daily food**, through your life **bound to the Two Hearts** and linked to souls in need of her maternal help, by unbroken chains of Rosaries and continuous acts of mercy and love, all united with the Eucharistic Lord, **all in the Divine Will**. Our Lady is asking us to offer our lives to delay and possibly even prevent some of the prevailing evil and divine justice that is to come and to help save souls who cannot save themselves. As **Our Lady of Akita** says:

> *I have prevented the coming of calamities by offering to the Father, together with all the **victim souls** who console Him, the sufferings endured by the Son on the Cross, by His Blood and by His very loving Soul. Prayer, penance, and courageous sacrifices can appease the anger of the Father.*

What is needed is *your* prayer, penance, and courageous sacrifices – consecrated to the Two Hearts, in the Divine Will – to defeat Satan and to save the world! To usher in the New Kingdom! An army of victims of love, even if small, is needed to combat the apostasy, heresy, and compromises, which are currently challenging the Faith. This army will march forward with *joy and love* offering all to Jesus through Mary. These faithful ones will be the greatest power of this age. And assuredly, we will thank Jesus for the sacrifices that He has made us do! About this, **Our Lady of Good Success** says:

> The **small number of souls, who hidden, will preserve the treasures of the Faith and practice virtue** *will suffer a cruel, unspeakable and prolonged martyrdom. Many will succumb to death from the violence of their sufferings and those who sacrifice themselves for the Church and their country will be counted as martyrs. In order to free men from the bondage to these heresies, those whom the merciful love of my most Holy Son has designated* **to effect the restoration**, *will need great strength of will, constancy, valor, and confidence in God. There will be occasions when all will seem lost and paralyzed. This then will be* **the happy beginning of the complete restoration**.

As too **Luisa Piccarreta** foresaw, saying:

> *And precisely in this century, so troubled,* **the Lord is preparing a new era**, *which will invade His Church and all men of good will, and in which the triumph of Grace will be the ultimate goal… [So, let us take courage as Jesus reminds us:]* **Do not fear**; *I will be with you until the end of time.*

In the new Kingdom that is unfolding before us even now, His Divine Will will be done by all at last. And only His Will can ensure peace among His children. In the new Kingdom, all people will love Him, accept His Love and Gifts, which He wishes to shower upon His children, and live in communion with Him and each other. The final battle that has already begun will see the destruction of evil being finally completed and ultimately itself destroyed. With it shall come the triumph and reign of the Two Hearts, the Era of Peace, and the coming Kingdom of the Divine Will on earth as it is in Heaven.

Though now is the time of great and sorrowful tribulations, it is necessary that all of this occur so that the Lord can bring about the Great Victory, which will bring peace to the whole world. Soon – at that time, Jesus will wipe away your tears and you will experience a great time of peace. Seek Jesus in the Eucharist and Our Lady thorough living the Consecration – say only *"yes"*. **Be filled with hope.** Live in the Divine Will and you will be guided and led to the greatest holiness. Do not be discouraged. Humanity will find peace, the Immaculate Heart will triumph, the Sacred Heart will reign, and the Kingdom of the Divine Will will come – through you, simple souls who are meek and humble of heart. And as we long for His appearance, knowing ourselves, we can only say: *"O God, be merciful to me a sinner."* For, what a glorious future awaits us! **Have hope!**

YOU Are the Apostles of the End Times

In his *True Devotion to Mary*, **St. Louis de Montfort** prophesies about the great Marian Saints of the latter times, in our times, who will form a spiritual army consecrated to Mary acting as her instrument in defeating the Devil and his Antichrist, saying to us:

> *[The] great saints who shall surpass most of the other saints in sanctity... full of grace and zeal, [these holy persons] shall be chosen to match themselves against the enemies of God,*

*who shall rage on all sides; and they shall be singularly devoted to our Blessed Lady, illuminated by her light, strengthened by her nourishment, led by her spirit, supported by her arm and sheltered under her protection... they shall fight, overthrow and crush the heretics with their heresies, the schismatics with their schisms, the idolaters with their idolatries and the sinners with their impieties... they **shall draw the whole world to true devotion to Mary**... It is through Mary that the salvation of the world was begun, and **it is through Mary that it must be consummated**... in order that, through her, **Jesus Christ** may be known, loved and served... God, then, wishes to reveal and make known Mary, the masterpiece of His hands, in these latter times... [Satan] **fears her** not only more than all angels and men, but in a sense more than God Himself... because Satan, being proud, suffers infinitely more from being beaten and punished by a little and humble handmaid of God [and] because God has given Mary such great power against the devils... **the power of Mary over the devils** will especially shine forth in the latter times, when Satan will lay his snares against her heel: that is to say, **her humble slaves and her poor (spiritual) children**, whom she will raise up to make war against him. They shall be little and poor in the world's esteem [but] they shall be rich in the grace of God... in union with Mary, they shall crush the head of the devil and cause Jesus Christ to triumph... [These holy persons] **will consecrate themselves*** *entirely to her service as subjects and slaves of love... They will know that she is the surest, the easiest, the shortest and the most perfect means of going to Jesus Christ; and they will give themselves to Mary, body and soul, without reserve, that they may thus belong entirely to Jesus Christ... like burning fire [they]* **shall kindle the fire of divine love** *everywhere... [And] detaching themselves from everything and troubling themselves about nothing, [they] shall shower forth the rain of the Word of God and of eternal life. They shall thunder against sin; they shall storm against the world; they shall strike the devil and his crew... They shall be the true* **apostles of the latter times**... *they shall be true disciples of Jesus Christ, walking in the footsteps of His poverty, humility, contempt of the world, charity; teaching the narrow way of God in pure truth, according to the holy Gospel... [and]* **Mary is the one who, by order of the Most High, shall fashion them for the purpose of extending His empire over that of the impious, the idolaters and the Muslims.**

Are *you* listening? Do you hear your calling? **Our Lady of La Salette** is likewise asking you to take up *your mission*, to join *"the Apostles of the Last Days, the faithful disciples of Jesus Christ who have lived in scorn for the world and for themselves, in poverty and in humility, in scorn and in silence, in prayer and in mortification, in chastity and in union with God, in suffering and unknown to the world. It is time [you] came out and filled the world with light... (She says,)* **Fight, children of light**, *you, the few who can see. For now is the time of all times, the* *end of all ends."* With Our Lady's help, remain true to Jesus' teachings and pray for His protection and mercy. If you surrender to Him, asking His guidance, listening to His prophecies, all will be well!

The Final Victory Awaits

In the Second Coming of Christ, the righteous will reign with Christ forever. The Book of Revelation states: ***"He will wipe away every tear from their eyes, and death shall be no more, neither shall there be mourning nor crying nor pain any more, for the former things have passed away"*** (21:4). And Christ will declare to the faithful: *"Blessed are those who wash their robes (in faith and righteous deeds of love), that they may have the right to the tree of life and that they may enter the city... The Spirit and the Bride say, 'Come'"* (22:14, 17). God in Heaven is making ready!

So now, how are you going to respond? You have received the heavenly Message of the Grace of all graces, which is the invitation to live in the Divine Will. And God has called you to receive the Gift of entering the New Ark, which is Our Lady's Immaculate Heart. To those who are given much, much is now expected. So, where are you going from here? It cannot be business as usual, not for you, not now that you have received this Grace and Gift. As Our Lady's warriors of love, truth, and peace, **you must fight or die.** In this book, God has given you both His battle plan and the assurance of how to achieve victory. Pray! Prayer is your weapon. Prayer will provide you with the armor you need to defeat the evil one. Prayer will dilute the impact of war, suffering, and every kind of persecution being planned by the enemies of God. Prayer will save you and all those for whom you pray. And when the New Dawn of victory comes, you will cry tears of joy when you will be shown the fruits of your prayer. Pray, pray, pray!

Forward now, toward victory! *"Keep the commandments without stain or reproach, until the appearance of our Lord Jesus Christ at the proper time, the King of kings and Lord of lords"* (1 Timothy 6:15). And do so having the eternal reward in sight: that for you on the day this great battle ends, which is not far from now, when the Immaculate Heart will triumph and the Sacred Heart will reign anew, Christ will come again and declare, before all the Angels and Saints, to you: *"Well done, my good and faithful friend. Now, enter into the Kingdom of the Divine Will, you and the millions you have helped to save."* **You will meet Him mystically in the New Kingdom**, and the two of you will throw yourselves into each other's arms, you embracing Him and He embracing you in a united embrace of victory. **And Our Blessed Mother, being there spiritually as well to take you into her arms**, will say to you: *"I am proud of you, my child, because you, among the so very few who responded to my call, gave your life for the good of all. Thank you. With your help, we have won. The Great Victory is ours indeed."* Go to Mary! Is she not your Mother? Has she not promised to protect you? Yes, yes! Thus, be always encouraged by the words of the *Memorare*, given to us by **St. Bernard of Clairvaux**, saying: *"Never was it known that anyone who fled to her protection, implored her help or sought her intercession was left unaided."* Thus, all will be blessed.

The moment to fight is now. And the place to fight is here. The way to fight is to be a sign of contradiction to the ways of the world and our times! Let us joyfully love, even our enemies, in this time of selfishness; faithfully obey and defend the teachings of the Church in this modern atmosphere of rebellion and excessive toleration; courageously be merciful to a world that demands revenge; boldly trust in the Lord when all around you place their trust in themselves, pleasure-seeking and idols; daringly remain hopeful in this climate of despair; and fearlessly pray while clinging to the Lord, *"not fearing the terror of the night nor the arrow that flies by day... **though a thousand may fall at your side**, ten thousand at your right hand; but it will not come near you... and the punishment of the wicked you will see. [For the Lord promises that] no evil shall befall you, no scourge come near your house. **He will give His angels charge over you** to guard you in all your ways, who will bear you up lest you dash your foot against a stone... and **the dragon you will trample under foot"*** (Psalm 91). Thus, truly Jesus says to you today: *"**Blessed are you** who keep this <u>prophetic message</u>"* (Rev 22:7) from Heaven for our times.

Yes, victory is assured! And the Grace of all graces has now been given! The New Ark has descended! And God has chosen *you* to join Jesus and His Mother in this the great battle, which is fully upon us now... Can you see it? **The Great Victory is just on the horizon**, where *"the righteous will shine like the sun in the kingdom of their Father"* (Matthew 13:43)! Fight bravely, and never give up, until united again, we can all together say, *"Alleluia! God has been victorious. The battle is over. And we have won! The new day of the Kingdom of the Divine Will, on earth as it is in Heaven, has dawned."* Thus, arise; the hour is late, let us be on our way! *Couragio!*

ABOUT THE AUTHOR

Dr. Kelly Bowring, received his masters in theology and Christian ministry, with advanced certification in catechetics, from Franciscan University of Steubenville, his licentiate in sacred theology from Dominican House of Studies (and the John Paul II Institute) in Washington, DC, and his pontifical doctorate in sacred theology from the Pontifical University of St. Thomas Aquinas in Rome.

Dr. Bowring has received the theological *mandatum* to teach theology. He previously taught theology and directed an institute at St. Mary's College of Ave Maria University, and he has been a professor of sacred theology at Southern Catholic College, where he was the Dean of Spiritual Mission and oversaw the theology program. He also served as Dean of the "Graduate School of Theology" (GST) at St. Charles Borromeo Seminary.

Dr. Bowring has published several books including *The Secrets, Chastisement, and Triumph*; *The Great Battle Has Begun*; *Dear Children, The Messages of Our Lady of Medjugorje* (with Vince Murray); and *To Hold and Teach the Catholic Faith* (St. Paul/Alba House) and various liturgical and prayer books with W. J. Hirten Publisher. His new book, *Your Life Redeemed*, is also being published with Two Hearts Press, LLC.

Dr. Bowring and his wife, Diana, have eight children.

For more information, go to our website: www.TwoHeartsPress.com

Email your comments or reviews about this book to:
TwoHeartsPressLLC@aol.com

TO ORDER these related books from Dr. Kelly Bowring, go to www.TwoHeartsPress.com or call (24/7) 800-BookLog (266-5564).

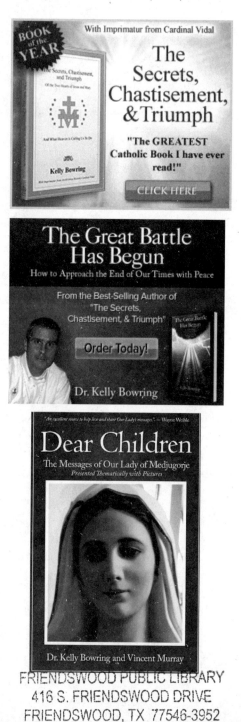